BEHOLD!
The Word of God

Kyle Butt

APOLOGETICS PRESS

Apologetics Press, Inc.

230 Landmark Drive
Montgomery, Alabama 36117-2752

© Copyright 2007
ISBN-10: 1-60063-002-2
ISBN-13: 978-1-60063-002-6
Printed in China

Library of Congress Cataloging-in-Publication
Kyle Butt (1976 -)
Behold! The Word of God
Includes bibliographic references
ISBN-10: 1-60063-002-2
ISBN 13: 978 1 60063 002 6
1. Bible. 2. Comparative religion. 3. Christian theology I. Title

220—dc22   2007929966

DEDICATION

To Eric Lyons, my friend and co-worker, whose positive influence on my life has helped me to understand the proverb—"As iron sharpens iron, so a man sharpens the countenance of his friend" (Proverbs 27:17).

ACKNOWLEDGEMENTS

I would like to thank Wayne Jackson for graciously allowing me to include his material on Babylon. His research and generous, godly attitude have been an inspiration to me in my writing. Also, special thanks to my colleagues Dave Miller and Eric Lyons who allowed me to use portions of their materials. Their kind dispositions help make my work at Apologetics Press one of the genuine joys of my life.

TABLE OF CONTENTS

CHAPTER 1

THE BIBLE'S CLAIM OF INSPIRATION

In America, as well as many countries all over the world, the Bible is the most popular book that has ever been printed. It has been translated in whole or in part into over 2,000 different languages ("About the Bible," 2005). The Bible was one of the first books mass produced on Gutenberg's printing press in 1455 ("Johann Gutenberg," 2006). In a single year over 585 million Bibles or sections of the Bible were distributed worldwide by the United Bible Society alone ("Worldwide Scripture," 1999). To estimate a total number of Bibles and portions of it that have been produced and distributed worldwide throughout history would be virtually impossible, but the number stands well over tens of billions, since the United Bible Society alone has distributed over nine billion since 1947 ("God Facts," n.d.). Without dispute, the Bible is the best-selling book of all time ("Best Selling...," 2002). About 90% of American households have at least one copy of the Bible.

In truth, the Bible has smashed every statistical record ever devised in regard to numbers published, printed, and distributed. The Bible has proven itself to be a timeless resource that crosses all geographic and generational barriers. For hundreds of years, witnesses in judicial proceedings have sworn (or affirmed) to tell the truth with their right hands on the Bible. More Bible verses have been quoted by United States Presidents in their public speeches than all other books combined. The Bible speaks to the deepest yearnings of mankind, answers the most difficult philosophical questions, and comforts the most downtrodden spirits. The practical, every-day advice from this magnificent book has been the foundation for countless best-selling self-help books and seminars.

Why is the Bible so popular and pervasive? The primary reason given in response to this question is that the Bible is God's Word. Millions of people print, purchase, read, and reread the Bible because they believe that the book they are reading is actually a product of the one true God.

Oftentimes, when people are asked to prove that the Bible is from God, they offer as "proof" the fact that the Bible **claims** to be from God. Anyone who reads the Bible cannot help but be impressed with the fact that the Bible is replete with statements that suggest that it is a product from God. Second Timothy 3:16 states: "All Scripture is given by inspiration of God...." In fact, were a person to search the entire Bible, he or she would discover that it contains approximately 3,000 instances that claim inspiration. A quick perusal of the Old Testament book of Jeremiah uncovers the fact that, in this one book, inspiration is claimed over 500 times by the use of such phrases as: "Then the word of the Lord came to me, saying" (1:4;

2:1); "Hear the word of the Lord" (2:4); "The Lord said also to me" (3:6); "For thus says the Lord to the men of Judah and Jerusalem" (4:3); "Says the Lord" (5:19). This list of inspiration claims in the book of Jeremiah could literally fill several pages. Other books such as Isaiah, Ezekiel, Psalms, and Micah, to name a few, are similarly packed with such claims.

New Testament writers, as well, insist that their writings are not the product of human invention, but instead are the work of God. In writing to the Thessalonians, Paul stated: "For this reason we also thank God without ceasing, because when you received the word of God which you heard from us, you welcomed it not as the word of men, **but as it is in truth, the word of God,** which also effectively works in you who believe" (1 Thessalonians 2:13, emp. added). Similar sentiments flowed from Paul's pen in his first letter to the Corinthians, in which he wrote: "If anyone thinks himself to be a prophet or spiritual, let him acknowledge that the things which I write to you are the commandments of the Lord" (1 Corinthians 14:37). The apostle Peter also attributed inspirational status to the writings of Paul when he included Paul's writings in connection with the "rest of the Scriptures" (2 Peter 3:16). Peter further included the commandments of the apostles in with the words "which were spoken before by the holy prophets" as inspired commandments and teachings (2 Peter 3:1-3). It certainly cannot be denied that the Bible **claims** to be inspired by God.

Yet, even though one would expect to find that any book truly produced by God would claim such inspiration, such a claim does not necessarily prove anything.

It is a necessary trait of inspiration, but it is not a sufficient trait. Several other books claim to be inspired by God, but are contradictory to the books found in the Bible, and can be proven to be inaccurate and deficient in multiple categories. Just because a book or particular writing claims inspiration is not positive proof of its inspiration. Any person could stand in front of an audience and claim to be the president of the United States of America. In fact, he could fill many hours claiming such to be the case in a multitude of diverse ways. But his multiple claims to the presidency would utterly fail to prove his case unless he could provide more adequate and sufficient evidence for his claim.

Sadly, most of those individuals who consider themselves to be Christians have never taken their defense of the Bible past the statement that it claims to be God's Word. When asked why they believe that the Bible is God's Word, they site passages like 2 Timothy 3:16-17 or 2 Peter 1:20-21 and insist that the case is closed. When they are shown that such does not sufficiently prove the Bible's inspiration, they often are at a loss for additional evidence that verifies the Bible's divine origin.

In fact, when confronted with the fact that biblical claims of inspiration are insufficient proof, many Christians say that the Bible's inspiration must be accepted by "faith." By the term "faith," most people in the religious world mean the acceptance of the claim without sufficient evidence to prove it. Even *Webster's Dictionary* gives one definition of faith as a "firm belief in something for which there is no proof" ("Faith"). To accept this idea, however, lands the adherent in complete confusion. If one is to accept the Bible's inspiration by "faith" (without adequate evidence), what would stop the Mormon practitioner from demanding that the *Book of Mormon* and *The Pearl of Great Price* should be considered inspired based on "faith"? The same could be said for the Quran, Hindu Vedas, and several other writings that claim inspiration. If "by faith" is meant that adequate evidence is not necessary to establish the claim, then any book in the world could be considered inspired "by faith."

In most instances, when a person says that the Bible's inspiration should be accepted by "faith" (without supporting evidence), that person believes that he is recapitulating the Bible's own statements regarding the necessity of having faith (see Hebrews 11:6). The problem lies, however, in the discordant definitions of faith. The biblical definition of faith never has embodied the idea of accepting or believing something without adequate evidence. On the contrary, when Bible writers demand "faith" from their readers, they are demanding that the readers draw only those conclusions that are warranted by the evidence.

The showdown between Elijah and the prophets of Baal on Mount Carmel provides the perfect case-in-point (1 Kings 18:20-40). Elijah had summoned Ahab and all the people of Israel to Mount Carmel. He then said to the multitude of people, "How long will you falter between two opinions? If the Lord is God, follow Him; but if Baal, then follow Him" (18:21). Elijah then proposed a contest in which the 450 prophets of Baal would be given a bull and he would be given one as well. Each "team" would be allowed to put the bull on an altar prepared for a sacrifice. No fire, however, would be given to either group. It was the responsibility of Baal or Jehovah God to produce fire. The God who sent fire from heaven would be the true God and would warrant the worship of the Israelites. The evidence for belief, in this case, was fire coming from heaven. The prophets of Baal begged for fire, but none was forthcoming. Elijah prayed for fire to consume his sacrifice and that is exactly what happened (18:37-38). The people present at this showdown then concluded, "The Lord, He is God!" (18:39).

This account concerning Elijah is not interjected in this book as a proof of biblical inspiration. It is rather introduced as evidence that those who wrote the Bible never asked their readers to believe in God, or the authenticity of His Word (which they were writing and speaking), **without adequate evidence**.

The Bible writers insisted that their writings were not based on imaginary, nonverifiable people and events, but were instead grounded on solid, verifiable facts. The apostle Peter, in his second epistle, wrote: "For we did not follow cunningly devised fables when we made known to you the power and coming of our Lord Jesus Christ, but were eyewitnesses of His majesty" (1:16). In a similar statement, the apostle John insisted: "That which was from the beginning, which we have heard, which we have seen with our eyes, which we have looked upon, and our hands have handled, concerning the Word of life.... [T]hat which we have seen and heard we declare to you, that you also may have fellowship with us" (1 John 1:1,3).

When Luke wrote his account of the Gospel of Christ, he specifically and intentionally crafted his introduction to ensure that his readers understood that his account was historical and factual:

> Inasmuch as many have taken in hand to set in order a narrative of those things which have been fulfilled among us, just as those who from the beginning were eyewitnesses and ministers of the word delivered them to us, it seemed good to me also, having had perfect understanding of all things from the very first, to write to you an orderly account, most excellent Theophilus, that you may know the certainty of those things in which you were instructed (Luke 1:1-4).

In a similar line of reasoning, Luke included in his introduction to the book of Acts the idea that Jesus "presented Himself alive after His suffering by many infallible proofs, being seen by them during forty days and speaking of the things pertaining to the kingdom of God" (Acts 1:3).

In addition, when the apostle Paul argued the case that Jesus Christ had truly been raised from the dead, he wrote that the resurrected Jesus

> was seen by Cephas, then by the twelve. After that He was seen by over five hundred brethren at once, of whom the greater part remain to the present, but some have fallen asleep. After that He was seen by James, then by all the apostles. Then last of all He was seen by me also, as by one born out of due time (1 Corinthians 15:5-8).

This handful of verses reveals that the Bible writers insisted with conviction that their writings were not mythical, but were indeed based on factual events. Furthermore, they specifically documented many proofs that could be assessed to determine the accuracy of their statements. The evidence is overwhelming that the Bible writers understood and insisted that their information was accurate and factual, and should be accepted, not based on a lack of evidence or a "leap in the dark," but instead based on an abundance of documentable, verifiable proof.

Having dismissed, then, the idea that the Bible's inspiration should be accepted by "faith" (without adequate evidence), it will be the purpose of the remainder of this book to supply such evidence as would lead an unbiased, honest observer to the conclusion that the Bible is the product of a divine Mind.

CHAPTER 2

INSPIRATION DEFINED

One of the first steps that must be taken in any discussion is to identify key terms and define them. Since the term "inspiration" is obviously one of the key terms in this discussion, what does it mean? The word is defined by *Merriam-Webster* as: "a divine influence or action on a person believed to qualify him or her to receive and communicate sacred revelation" ("Inspiration," n.d.). When the New Testament writer, Peter, discussed inspiration, he noted that "holy men of God spoke **as they were moved** by the Holy Spirit" (2 Peter 1:21, emp. added). The New International Version translates the phrase "carried along." In 1 Thessalonians, Paul commented that the Word he was speaking was not the word of men, "but as it is in truth, the word of God" (1 Thessalonians 2:13). Inspiration, then, means that the actual human writers were "carried" or "moved" by the divine Author to communicate His message.

FURTHER NARROWING OF THE DEFINITION OF BIBLICAL INSPIRATION

The idea that the holy men of God were moved by the Holy Spirit must yet be qualified further. Did these men communicate ideas in their own words? Did they include additional information from their own ideas? Is the entire Bible inspired, or does it contain certain non-inspired sections as well? These questions and others similar to them hinge on the biblical definition of "inspiration."

Word-for-Word Inspiration

Several times in the Bible, an argument is made by one of the writers or speakers that hinges on the accuracy of a single word in the biblical text. For instance, when Paul wrote to the Galatians, he tried to show them that Christ was the Seed of Abraham through Whom the entire world would be blessed. Paul stated: "Now to Abraham and his Seed were the promises made. He does not say, 'And to seeds,' as of many, but as of one, 'And to your Seed,' who is Christ" (3:16). Paul's entire argument rests on the fact that the Old Testament passage he is quoting has the word "seed" in the singular form and not the plural form. From this fact, it is evident that Paul considered even such a minor difference in the number of a noun as an important, inspired (divinely ordered) difference that could be trusted and used as evidence.

In a similar way, Jesus made arguments based on word order or tense. On one occasion, the Sadducees approached Jesus in an attempt to trap Him in His words. Since they did not believe in the resurrection of the dead, they posed a scenario which they thought was sure to catch Jesus in some type of error. They presented the case of a woman who had seven husbands during the course of her life. "In the resurrection," they asked, "whose wife of the seven will she be?" Jesus proceeded to explain to them that they did not understand the Scriptures or the power of God. In the resurrection, humans would neither marry nor be married. As evidence of the reality of life after death, Jesus quoted a section of Scripture from Exodus 3, in which God stated: "I am the God of Abraham, the God of Isaac, and the God of Jacob" (emp. added). Jesus then concluded that "God is not the God of the dead, but of the living" (Matthew 22:23-33). How could Jesus conclude that God is the God of the living, even though Abraham, Isaac, and Jacob had been dead for many years prior to God's conversation with Moses?

The answer lies in the tense of the verb recorded in the text. God did not say "I was" the God of Abraham, or "I will be" the God of Isaac. God stated that at the present "I am" the God of these patriarchs, meaning that even though their earthly lives had ended, they continued to exist and God continued to be their God. [NOTE: The claim that Jesus made arguments based even on the tense of verbs is true. Nevertheless, such a statement needs clarification. Hebrew actually has no past, present, or future tense. Rather, an action is regarded as being either complete or incomplete, and so verbs occur in the Hebrew as perfect or imperfect. No verb occurs in God's statement in Exodus 3:6. Consequently, tense is implied rather than expressed. In this case, the Hebrew grammar would allow any tense of the verb "to be." Jesus, however, clarified the ambiguity inherent in the passage by affirming specifically what God had in mind, which is why Matthew preserved Jesus' use of the Greek present tense (*ego eimi*).]

From these two instances, it is clear that not only are the ideas of the Bible writers inspired, but even the very words used were a product of divine guidance–down to the tense of a verb or number of a noun.

This word-for-word, or verbal, inspiration does not imply divine dictation in which the writers were nothing more than human typewriters. In fact, anyone familiar with the Bible can bring to mind several instances in which an individual writer's personal writing style or unique experiences are recorded. For instance, in the book of Philippians, Paul made several allusions to personal interactions that he enjoyed with the Philippians. He mentioned that their messenger, Epaphroditus, had safely arrived with the gift sent by the church there. Furthermore, Paul noted several helpers who had done a part to aid him in furthering the Gospel, including Euodia, Syntyche, and Clement. Obviously, Paul's interactions with these people were real and personal. Verbal (word-for-word) inspiration does not mean that the writers could never include personal information or unique writing style. It does mean that the Holy Spirit guided the writers to include only the information that would be relevant to the gospel message in some way, and only in the words permitted by the Holy Spirit.

Complete Inspiration

Another paramount aspect of biblical inspiration is the idea that the Bible contains the entire Word of God, without additional, humanly devised material. This was Peter's point when he wrote that "no prophecy of Scripture is of any private interpretation" (or origin–KB) (2 Peter 1:20). It is not the case that the Bible **contains** the Word of God, or that His Word must be filtered out from other, non-inspired material inserted by the Bible writers. Paul stated that "**all** Scripture is given by inspiration of God" (2 Timothy 3:16, emp. added). According to the biblical idea of inspiration, the Bible, in its entirety, is the Word of God. The psalmist wrote: "The entirety of Your word is truth, and every one of Your righteous judgments endures forever" (Psalm 119:160).

Many modern liberal scholars have suggested that some parts of the Bible are not the product of divine inspiration, but instead are simply human opinions or stories inserted by the Bible writers to make the book more interesting or relevant. This type of thinking lands the adherent in a hopeless mess. Which parts of Scripture, then, are to be taken as inspired and which are to be deemed as human invention? One quickly realizes that the answer to that question basically consists of the idea that whatever information the liberal scholar likes or agrees with happens to be inspired, and what he or she does not like "must be" human invention. In truth, the biblical definition of "inspiration" includes the idea that all Scripture is inspired, and that the Bible writers did not "insert" anything into the text on their own.

The idea of "complete" (or plenary) inspiration can also entail the concept that the Bible is all that is now needed in order for a human to understand God's will. In John 16, Jesus informed His apostles that He had many things to tell them that they simply were not yet ready to handle. He then promised to send "the Spirit of truth" Who would guide them "into all truth" (16:13). On another occasion, Jesus encouraged His apostles to be aware that they would be delivered up to leaders who would abuse them and persecute them. When this happened, Jesus instructed the men not to "worry about how or what you should speak, for it will be given to you in that hour what you should speak; for it is not you who speak, but the Spirit of your Father who speaks in you" (Matthew 10:19-20). In Acts 1:25-2:4, the text records the fact that the Holy Spirit came upon the apostles and they immediately were "moved" to preach the Word of God. Throughout the book of Acts, the apostles and other inspired men made statements, preached sermons, and wrote epistles that laid out God's plan of salvation for mankind. In one of his epistles, the apostle Peter noted that commandments which were spoken by the apostles were just as authoritative as the words spoken "by the holy prophets" (2 Peter 3:2). Peter further noted that the writings of Paul were inspired and deserved their place alongside "the rest of the Scriptures" (2 Peter 3:16).

According to the New Testament, everything necessary for human salvation has been recorded and included in the Scriptures. Peter verified this statement when he wrote that God's divine power "has given to us all things that pertain to life and godliness" (2 Peter 1:3). Paul's statement to Timothy includes these sentiments as well, since he stated that the Scriptures were enough to make the man of God "complete, thoroughly equipped for every good work" (2 Timothy 3:17). Furthermore, Paul noted that even an angel from heaven would be cursed if he preached to the Galatians any other Gospel than the one that they had received (Galatians 1:8-10).

The biblical definition of inspiration, then, is the idea that the Holy Spirit moved the Bible writers to pen the words that He wanted, but allowed them to maintain their own unique style and personal experiences that fit the message. Furthermore, this text is complete in that it is God's Word in its entirety, without additional, uninspired information by the biblical writers. And it is complete in that it contains God's entire plan for human salvation without the need for additional inspired materials. [NOTE: The verbal, plenary inspiration of the Bible applies to the original message that the writers penned in the autographs of their works—an autograph being the actual, original letter or book produced by the Bible writer. The next chapter deals with the transmission of the text from the original autographs to the present.]

CHAPTER 3

BIBLE TRANSMISSION

When we open the Bible, we are reading from a catalog of 66 books, some of which were written more than 3,400 hundred years ago. The latest books of the New Testament were completed by 100 A.D., almost 2,000 years ago. How do we know that the original message penned by the writers of the Bible is the message that has been preserved in the Bible that we read today? Members of various world religions have suggested that the text of the Bible might have originally been inspired by God, but that message has been corrupted over the many centuries of copying and transmission. They would suggest that the books we now have may contain some inspired material, but non-inspired material has inevitably seeped into the text.

This allegation that the Bible has not been transmitted accurately, however, simply cannot be honestly upheld in light of the available evidence. In fact, entire books have been written detailing the evidence that verifies the accurate transmission of the biblical text. This chapter will provide a brief overview of such evidence. [NOTE: For a readable, yet scholarly treatment of the subject see Lightfoot's excellent volume *How We Got the Bible,* 2003.]

Stone

In the past, a medium was needed that could contain written material that would last an extended period of time. Furthermore, the material needed to be abundant and easily accessible to those who would be using it. Stone provided just such material. The supply of stone was virtually inexhaustible, and information carved into it would be lastingly set and preserved. For these reasons, stone was used in the past as a popular medium for transmitting written messages, including certain portions of the biblical text. Neil Lightfoot notes that the Babylonian code of Hammurabi was engraved in stone. This set of legal codes was written about 1750 B.C. Lightfoot further explains: "The oldest substantial portions of Hebrew writing found in Palestine are also on stone. The best examples of these are the Gezer Calendar and the Siloam inscription" (2003, p. 13). Other famous stone inscriptions include such archaeological treasures as the Rosetta stone, which was discovered in 1799. This remarkable discovery was instrumental in deciphering the ancient Egyptian language of hieroglyphics (Wegner, 1999, p. 91).

When we turn to the biblical text, we find that certain portions of the Old Testament, such as the Ten Commandments, were engraved in stone. Exodus 34:1 states: "And the Lord said to Moses, 'Cut two tablets of stone like the first ones, and I will write on these tablets the words that were on the first tablets.'" In addition, Moses instructed the elders of Israel to gather stones, whitewash them, and "write very plainly on the stones all the words of this law" (Deuteronomy 27:8).

Naturally, however, stone writing tablets would have inherent qualities that would pose difficulties for scribes. First, stone would be very heavy and would not be easily transported. It would do well for sedentary inscription, but messages that required more mobility would be difficult to transport. Furthermore, the chiseling process often used to inscribe stone was arduous and time consuming. In addition, the inflexible nature of stone resulted in the destruction of many tablets by shattering—as is recorded in Exodus 32:19. For these reasons, ancient people looked for other materials on which to write.

Clay

Since stone often required considerable time to engrave, the ancients turned to a medium that could be engraved more quickly—clay. Clay possessed many qualities that made it suitable writing material. It was common, inexpensive, and easy to engrave. Furthermore, once the clay dried, the words engraved in it became permanently set. Multiplied thousands of ancient writings have been discovered carved into clay. In 1879, Hormoz Rasam discovered a now-famous clay cylinder (about nine inches long), upon which King Cyrus had inscribed his victory over the city of Babylon and his policy toward the nations he had captured (Price, 1997, pp. 251-252). Researchers have uncovered significant clay seals called bullae that contained the names of certain biblical characters (pp. 235-237). And in 1876, archaeologist Hugo Winkler helped discover an enormous cache of more than 10,000 clay tablets describing the life and times of the Hittite nation (p. 83). In addition, the prophet Ezekiel mentioned a clay tablet in 4:1: "You also, son of man, take a clay tablet and lay it before you, and portray on it a city, Jerusalem."

Although clay possessed several excellent traits that made it suitable for writing, it had drawbacks. Once dried, the text of clay could not easily be adjusted and the clay could not be reused. Furthermore, dried clay tablets could be quite brittle and would often break. In addition, since it is quite heavy, clay tablets or cylinders were not easy to transport.

Papyrus

Near shallow lakes and rivers grew a tall reed called papyrus. It especially grew by the Nile River in Egypt. The ancient people would harvest this hollow reed, slit it down the middle, and roll it out flat. Then they would glue the flattened reeds together. After gluing many of the reeds together, a rock was used to smooth the surface of the papyrus so that it could be written on like modern paper. The ink, made from plants or dyes, would be applied to the finished sheet using a sharp stick, quill, or other "pen-like" instrument. Miller and Huber explain that papyrus was one of the world's first inexpensive, durable writing mediums (2004, p. 20). In fact, many of the Dead Sea Scrolls, the oldest scrolls that contain portions of the Old Testament, were composed of papyrus (p. 20).

During the New Testament times, most of the manuscripts of New Testament books were papyrus documents. Lightfoot notes: "The popularity of papyrus spread from Egypt to surrounding countries, and its use was so general that it became the universal medium for the making of books in Greece and Rome. We are quite sure that the letters and books of the New Testament were written at first on papyrus" (2003, p. 18).

With the use of papyrus, much information could be carried at one time (unlike the use of clay and stone). Also, if a person dropped a papyrus scroll, it did not crack and break. Writing on papyrus was not difficult either; it did not take hours to engrave and dry. With all the advantages that came with the use of papyrus, certain disadvantages also presented themselves. Papyrus decayed easily and usually would not last as long as clay or stone. Much like paper, if it fell into water or if it was exposed to rain, it would be ruined. The advantages, however, far outweighed the disadvantages, and papyrus became a significant medium by which the New Testament documents were originally transmitted.

Leather

Parchment and vellum are the names given to animal skins that were used as "paper." These animal skins would be dried and polished with a stone. Some times the ancient writers dyed the skins purple and used gold ink to write on them. Leather was lightweight, did not decay as quickly as papyrus, and could be produced by anyone in the world (not just people who lived by the Nile). Because of its superior durability, the Jews stipulated in the Talmud that the Torah was to be copied onto animal skin (Lightfoot, 2003, p. 19). Several of the most important New Testament manuscripts are composed of vellum. The Vatican manuscript, a "rare gem" in that it "contains in Greek almost all of the Old and New Testaments," is written on 759 leaves of fine vellum (p. 38). The Sinaitic manuscript, another extremely important New Testament document, is composed of 393 leaves of vellum (p. 51).

Of course, other materials were used in the ancient past to transcribe information. Wood, ivory, bone, pottery, and shells are but a few of these additional materials. But the ones mentioned in this chapter were the most popular forms of writing materials upon which important aspects of the Bible's transmission have depended.

OLD TESTAMENT TRANSMISSION

Moses began to write the first books of the Old Testament almost 3,500 years ago. All of the original documents that Moses, Isaiah, Jeremiah, and the other Old Testament writers produced have been lost or destroyed. We have only copies of their writings. How do we know that the original books were copied correctly? Can we be sure that the book of Genesis that we read in the 21st century is the same book that God inspired Moses to write 3,500 years ago? Yes, we can be sure that the Old Testament we read today has been copied accurately.

Serious Scribes

Although scribes are mentioned in the Bible as far back as 1,000 B.C. (Samuel 8:17), history records three general periods of Jewish scribal tradition: (1) the period of Sopherim (from Ezra until c. A.D. 200); (2) the Talmudic period (A.D. 100 to 500); and (3) the period of the Massoretes (c. 500 to 950) (Geisler and Nix, 1986, p. 502). Jewish copyists were aware of the importance of their work and took it very seriously. Infinitely more important than students copying spelling words, cooks copying recipes, or secretaries copying a boss's memo, scribes believed that they were copying the Word of God. Even the important work of medical transcriptionists cannot compare with the copyists of old. McGarvey noted how copyists in the Talmudic period "adopted for themselves very minute regulations to preserve the purity of the sacred text" (McGarvey, 1886, 1:9).

Later, the Massoretes took even more stringent steps to insure top-quality manuscripts. With a deep reverence for the Scriptures, they went above and beyond the "call of duty," laboring under ultra-strict rules in order to make the most accurate copies possible. In his *Introduction to the Old Testament*, Professor R.K. Harrison addressed the approach of the Massoretes to the Scriptures and their professionalism, saying:

> They concerned themselves with the transmission of the consonantal text as they had received it [Hebrew has no vowels–KB], as well as with its pronunciation, on the basis that the text itself was inviolable and every consonant sacred.
>
> The detailed statistical work that the Massoretes undertook on each book included the counting of verses, words, and letters, establishing the middle of the book (a procedure which was useful in the case of bifid, or two-part, compositions) noting peculiarities of style, and other similar matters (1969, pp. 212-213, parenthetical item in orig.).

By taking such precautions in the copying of letters, words, and verses (by sections and books), it could be known if a word or letter had been omitted or added. Indeed, as Eddie Hendrix affirmed: "Such minute checks contributed to a high degree of copying accuracy" (1976, 93[14]:5). No other group of ancient copyists is more renowned than those of the Old Testament.

The Dead Sea Scrolls

The Dead Sea Scrolls make up one of the greatest archaeological discoveries of all times. In 1947, a number of ancient documents were found by accident in a cave on the northwest side of the Dead Sea. This collection of documents, which has become known as the Dead Sea Scrolls, was comprised of old leather and papyrus scrolls and fragments that had been rolled up in earthen jars for centuries. From 1949 to 1956, hundreds of Hebrew and Aramaic manuscripts and a few Greek fragments were found in surrounding caves, and are believed by scholars to have been written between 200 B.C. and the first half of the first century A.D. Some of the manuscripts were of Jewish apocryphal and pseudepigraphical writings (e.g., 1 Enoch, Tobit, and Jubilees); others are often grouped together as "ascetic" writings (miscellaneous books of rules, poetry, commentary, etc.). The most notable and pertinent group of documents found in the caves of Qumran near the Dead Sea is the collection of Old Testament books. Every book from the Hebrew Bible was accounted for among the scrolls except the book of Esther.

The Dead Sea Scrolls serve as strong evidence for the integrity of the Old Testament text. Prior to 1947, the earliest known Old Testament manuscripts dated only to about A.D. 1000. With the discovery of the Dead Sea Scrolls, Bible scholars have been able to compare the present day text with the text from more than 2,000 years ago. Textual critics have found that these ancient copies of Old Testament books are amazingly similar to the Massoretic text. Indeed, they serve as proof that the Old Testament text has been transmitted faithfully through the centuries. As Rene Paché concluded: "Since it can be demonstrated that the text of the Old Testament was accurately transmitted for the last 2,000 years, one may reasonably suppose that it had been so transmitted from the beginning" (1971, p. 191).

NEW TESTAMENT TRANSMISSION

Almost 1,900 years ago, God inspired the writers of the New Testament to pen their books and letters. The actual letters and books written by these men are known as "autographs." Some may wonder how Christians can be confident that we have God's Word today, when the original autographs are no longer available for our viewing. How can one know the Truth, if the Truth comes from copies of copies of copies of the autographs, many of which contain various transcriptional errors? Should we simply give up and declare that attempts at finding the Truth are futile?

It is highly unreasonable to think that truths can be learned only from autographs. Learning and forming beliefs based on reliable copies of various written documents, objects, etc. is a way of life. To conclude that a driver in a particular state could not learn to drive adequately without having in hand the **original** driving manual produced by the state years earlier is absurd. To assert that no one could measure the length of one yard without having the standard yard in hand from the National Institute of Standards and Technology is ridiculous. Even if the standard yard was lost, the millions of copies of the yard in existence today would be sufficient in finding (or measuring) exactly what a yard is. Consider the example McGarvey used of an autograph, which eventually was destroyed.

> A gentleman left a large estate entailed to his descendants of the third generation, and it was not to be divided until a majority of them should be of age. During the interval many copies of the will were circulated among parties interested, many of these being copies of copies. In the meantime the office of record in which the original was filed was burned with all its contents. When the time for division drew near, a prying attorney gave out among the heirs the report that no two existing copies were alike. This alarmed them all and set them busily at work to ascertain the truth of the report. On comparing copy with copy they found the report true, but on close inspection it was discovered that the differences consisted in errors in spelling or grammatical construction; some mistakes in figures corrected by the written numbers; and some other differences not easily accounted for; but that in none of the copies did these mistakes affect the rights of the heirs. In the essential matters for which the will was written the representations of all the copies were precisely the same. The result was that they divided the estate with perfect satisfaction to all, and they were more certain that they had executed the will of their grandfather than if the original copy had been alone preserved; for it might have been tampered with in the interest of a single heir; but

the copies, defective though they were, could not have been (1886, 1:17).

Every day, all around the world, individuals, groups, businesses, schools, etc. operate with the conviction that autographs are unnecessary to learn the truths within them. Copies of wills, articles, and books can be gathered, inspected, and scrutinized until new copies are published that virtually are identical to the original. "[A]ccurate communication is possible despite technical mistakes in copying" (Archer, 1982, p. 29). So it is with the Bible.

The New Testament Evidence
Compared to Other Ancient Books

How does the New Testament measure up when it is compared to other ancient writings? F.F. Bruce examined much of the evidence surrounding this question in his book, *The New Testament Documents–Are They Reliable?* As he and other writers (e.g., Metzger, 1968, p. 36; Geisler and Brooks, 1990, p. 159) have noted, there are over 5,300 manuscripts of the Greek New Testament in existence today, in whole or in part, that serve to corroborate the accuracy of the New Testament. The best manuscripts of the New Testament are dated at roughly A.D. 350, the most important of these being the Codex Vaticanus, "the chief treasure of the Vatican Library in Rome," the Codex Sinaiticus, which was purchased by the British from the Soviet government in 1933, and the Codex Alexandrinus (Bruce, 1953, p. 20). Additionally, the Chester Beatty papyri, made public in 1931, contain eleven codices, three of which contain most of the New Testament (including the gospel accounts). Two of these codices boast a date in the first half of the third century, while the third is dated in the last half of the same century (p. 21). The John Rylands Library claims even earlier evidence. A papyrus codex containing parts of John 18 dates to the time of Hadrian, who reigned from A.D. 117 to 138 (p. 21).

The available evidence makes it clear that the gospel accounts were accepted as authentic by the close of the second century (Guthrie, 1970, p. 24). They were complete (or substantially complete) before A.D. 100, with many of the writings circulating 20-40 years before the close of the first century (Bruce, 1953, p. 16). Linton remarked concerning the gospel accounts: "A fact known to all who have given any study at all to this subject is that these books were quoted, listed, catalogued, harmonized, cited as authority by different writers, Christian and Pagan, right back to the time of the apostles (1943, p. 39)."

Such an assessment is absolutely correct. In fact, the New Testament enjoys far more historical documentation than any other volume ever known. There are only 643 copies of Homer's *Iliad*, which is undeniably the most famous book of ancient Greece. No one doubts the text of Julius Caesar's *Gallic Wars*, but we have only ten copies of it, the earliest of which was made 1,000 years after it was written. To have such abundance of copies for the New Testament from within 70 years of their writing is nothing short of amazing (Geisler and Brooks, 1990, pp. 159-160).

In his work, *The New Testament Documents—Are They Reliable?*, Bruce offered more astounding comparisons. Livy wrote 142 books of Roman history, of which a mere 35 survive. The 35 known books are made manifest due to some 20 manuscripts, only one of which is as old as the fourth century. The *History of Thucydides*, another well-known ancient work, is dependent upon only eight manuscripts, the oldest of these being dated about A.D. 900 (along with a few papyrus manuscripts dated at the beginning of the Christian era). *The History of Herodotus* finds itself in a similar situation. "Yet no classical scholar would listen to an argument that the authenticity of Herodotus or Thucydides is in doubt because the earliest MSS [manuscripts–KB] of their works which are of any use to us are over 1,300 years later than the originals" (Bruce, 1953, pp. 20-21). Bruce thus declared: "It is a curious fact that historians have often been much readier to trust the New Testament records than have many theologians" (p. 19).

Early Patristic Writers

Many of us have listened to a preacher talk about the Bible. Sometimes, that preacher might quote a certain biblical passage. In order to quote the passage, he had to have read it or heard it sometime in the past. In the same way, there were many ancient preachers who quoted the Bible, just like preachers do today. These early preachers lived only a few years after the Bible was written, and they quoted from it quite often. For instance, Ignatius, who lived from A.D. 70-110, quoted from the books of Matthew, Acts, Romans, and several others. Another man, Polycarp, lived from A.D. 70-156. In chapter four of a letter he wrote to people who lived in Philippi, Polycarp stated that "the love of money is the root of all evils" (cf. 1 Timothy 6:10) and that "we brought nothing into the world, so we can carry nothing out" (cf. 1 Timothy 6:7). In chapter five of the same letter he wrote, "God is not mocked" (cf. Galatians 6:7) Later in chapter seven, he said: "For whosoever does not confess that Jesus Christ has come in the flesh is antichrist" (cf. 1 John 4:3).

Justin Martyr, another early "church father" who lived from approximately A.D. 100 to 165, quoted large sections of the New Testament. In his *First Apology,* chapter 15 opens with this quote: "Whosoever looketh upon a woman to lust after her, hath committed adultery with her already in his heart before God" (cf. Matthew 5:28). And, "If thy right eye offend thee, cut it out; for it is better for thee to enter into the kingdom of heaven with one eye, than, having two eyes, to be cast into everlasting fire" (cf. Matthew 5:29).

Irenaeus (A.D. 130-202), in *Against Heresies,* book 1, chapter 8, quoted Paul as saying, "and last of all, He appeared to me also, as to one born out of due time" (cf. 1 Corinthians 15:8). And in the same chapter, he quoted Jesus (cf. Matthew 26:39) as saying, "Father, if it be possible, let this cup pass from Me" (for an extensive catalog of the writings of the "church fathers" see Knight, 2002).

The list of names and quotes could go on for several pages. After researching the church fathers and their texts for several years, the eminent New Testament scholar, Bruce Metzger, wrote: "Indeed, so extensive are these citations that if all other sources for our knowledge of the text of the New Testament were destroyed, they would be sufficient alone in reconstructing practically the entire New Testament" (1968, p. 86).

If the ancient preachers who lived between A.D. 70-200 quoted extensively from the New Testament, it means that the New Testament had to be complete, already circulating among the Christians, and accepted as Scripture before they quoted it. It also means that we can compare the New Testament that we read in the 21st century to the quotes that such preachers produced in those early years. What we find when we compare the two is that they are virtually identical. As Linton correctly observed: "There is no room for question that the records of the words and acts of Jesus of Galilee came from the pens of the men who, with John, wrote what they had 'heard' and 'seen' and their hands had 'handled of the Word of life'" (1943, pp. 39-40).

CONCLUSION

The transmission of the Bible has been scrutinized and critically considered more than any ancient book in human history. The evidence for its faithful transmission has been brought forth in such a forceful way that any honest person who has studied it carefully is forced to admit that the message of the Bible in the 21st century is the message that was originally penned by the Bible writers in every relevant respect. Eminent Bible scholar Sir Frederic Kenyon once stated concerning the New Testament's transmission that it is a subject "of which the foundations now stand fast on a firm basis of ascertained historical fact, and on which the superstructure of religion may be built with the full hope and confidence that it rests on an authentic text" (1951, p. 369).

CHAPTER 4

THE UNITY OF THE BIBLE

Most people who read the Bible in the 21st century rarely stop to think about the 66 different books that compose the sacred Scriptures. Because the 66 books fit together so perfectly, it is easy to consider them to be one organic unit. The major themes and stories from Genesis, the first book of the Bible, flow through the remaining books, and their meanings and implications are developed throughout the entire biblical library. Because of its seamless unity, few take the time to consider that the 66 books of the Bible were written over a vast period of time by a host of writers. The first five books of the Old Testament were composed by Moses in about 1450 B.C. (see Lyons and Smith, 2003). Revelation, the last book of the New Testament, was written by John, the apostle of Jesus and brother of James, between the years 60-100 A.D. (see Guthrie, 1970, pp. 949-961). Thus, the composition of the entire library of 66 books spanned some 1,600 years.

During those years, the books of the Bible were penned by approximately 40 men of varying backgrounds, cultures, and educational status. The book of Amos was written by a herdsman from Tekoa (1:1).

Many of the Psalms were written by David, the shepherd-boy-turned-king. Ezra, "skilled scribe in the Law of Moses," penned the book that bears his name (7:6). Nehemiah, the butler to King Artaxerxes, wrote the Old Testament book named for him. King Solomon, renowned in the ancient world for his immense wisdom, penned the majority of the Proverbs and the entire books of Ecclesiastes and Song of Solomon. The apostle Paul, a man highly educated at the feet of the Jewish teacher Gamaliel, wrote 13 of the 27 New Testament books. Luke, the first-century physician, penned the gospel account that bears his name as well as the book of Acts. Other New Testament writers included John, Peter, and Matthew, who were fishermen with little formal education.

To say that the writers of the Bible were diverse would be an understatement. Yet, though their educational and cultural backgrounds varied extensively, and though many of them were separated by several centuries, the 66 books that compose the Bible fit together perfectly. To achieve such a feat by employing mere human ingenuity and wisdom would be impossible. In fact, it would be impossible from a human standpoint to gather the writings of 40 men from the **same** culture, with the **same** educational background, during the **same** time period, and get any thing close to the unity that is evident in the Bible. The Bible's unity is a piece of remarkable evidence that proves its divine origin. The remainder of this chapter will be devoted to showing several different aspects of the Bible's unity. [NOTE: One of the primary examples of the Bible's unity revolves around the Messianic prophecies contained in the Old Testament and their fulfillment in the New Testament. The Messianic theme underlies the entire text of the 66 books of the Bible, and is explored in more fully in chapter 10.]

UNITY OF NARRATIVE MATERIAL

Many of the Bible writers used historic narrative to record the events that were pertinent to their particular writings. Stories such as Noah's ark and the Flood, the ten plagues in Egypt, and Daniel being thrown to the lions are recognized even among those with little Bible knowledge. A systematic study of the 66 books of the Bible quickly reveals an amazing unity between these books when they deal with such narratives.

Noah's Flood

The historic narrative detailing the events of the global Flood of Noah provides an excellent example of the Bible's unity. In Genesis 6-9, Moses recorded the events surrounding the greatest physical catastrophic event in Earth history. In this story, God chose a man named Noah to build a huge ark designed to carry at least two of every kind of animal, eight humans (Noah, his wife, his three sons, and their wives—Genesis 7:13), and all necessary supplies. When Noah completed the construction of this amazing vessel, Genesis records that God sent a flood to cover the entire globe. The text says: "And the waters prevailed exceedingly on the earth, and all the high hills under the whole heaven were covered.... And all flesh died that moved on the earth: birds and cattle and beasts and every creeping thing that creeps on the earth, and every man" (Genesis 7:19-21). The worldwide Flood destroyed every creature that had the breath of life except those saved in the ark. These events were recorded by Moses in about 1450 B.C.

As we scan the remaining books of the Bible, we find perfect harmony in regard to the events surrounding Noah, his descendants, and the global Flood. In 1 Chronicles, the text suggests that Noah's three sons were Shem, Ham, and Japheth, exactly as Genesis 7:13 records (1:1). The prophet Isaiah also referred to Noah (chapter 54). In that text, the prophet recorded the words God spoke to the Israelites of Isaiah's day: "For this is like the waters of Noah to Me; for as I have sworn that the waters of Noah would no longer cover the earth, so have I sworn that I would not be angry with you, nor rebuke you" (54:9). The oath to which Isaiah referred is found in Genesis 9:11, where God said to Noah: "Thus I establish My covenant with you: Never again shall all flesh be cut off by the waters of the flood; never again shall there be a flood to destroy the earth." Remarkably, Isaiah's comment exhibits a perfect understanding and awareness of God's statement to Noah, yet the prophet's writings were separated from Moses' writing of the Pentateuch by more than 600 years. In addition, the prophet Ezekiel acknowledged the story of Noah when he recorded God's Word to the Israelites of his day: "'Or if I send a pestilence into that land and pour out My fury on it in blood, and cut off from it man and beast, even though Noah, Daniel, and Job were in it, as I live,' says the Lord God, 'they would deliver neither son nor daughter; they would deliver only themselves by their righteousness'" (14:19-20).

The books of the New Testament exhibit the same unity in regard to the story of Noah as those of the Old. Matthew records the words of Jesus regarding Noah: "But as the days of Noah were, so also will the coming of the Son of Man be. For as in the days before the flood, they were eating and drinking, marrying and giving in marriage, until the day that Noah entered the ark, and did not know until the flood came and took them all away, so also will the coming of the Son of Man be" (24:36-39). Notice the points of agreement between Jesus' statement and the Genesis record. Jesus said that Noah was the man who built the ark. He also said that a great flood destroyed "them all," referring to everyone outside the ark, exactly as the Genesis account described. In fact, even though Jesus did not go into great detail, every aspect of His statement agrees perfectly with the information recorded in the Old Testament regarding the Flood. Luke recorded a similar statement by Jesus in Luke 17:26-27, which is the parallel passage to Matthew 24:36-39. He exhibited additional unity with Genesis in that he recorded that Noah's son was Shem (Luke 3:36).

In Hebrews 11, the Bible writer stated: "By faith, Noah, being divinely warned of things not yet seen, moved with godly fear, prepared an ark for the saving of his household, by which he condemned the world and became heir of the righteousness which is according to faith" (11:7) This passage in Hebrews concurs with various other passages that show that Noah built an ark by which his family was saved. Additionally, the apostle Peter twice mentioned Noah and the global Flood. He stated: "...when once the Divine longsuffering waited in the days of Noah, while the ark was being prepared, in which a few, that is, eight souls, were saved through water" (1 Peter 3:20). He also said: "[I]f God did not spare the angels who sinned, but cast them down to hell and delivered them into chains of darkness, to be reserved for judgment; and did not spare the ancient world, but saved Noah, one of eight people, a preacher of righteousness, bringing in the flood on the world of the ungodly" (2 Peter 2:5). Notice several things about Peter's comments regarding Noah. First, he records that Noah was the man who built the ark. Then he gives the exact number of people who were saved in that ark—eight. This number corresponds perfectly with the statement in Genesis 7:13 in which Moses said that Noah, his wife, his three sons, and their wives were saved. Furthermore, Peter states that the Flood destroyed the "ungodly." His description of the lifestyle of those destroyed in the Flood perfectly matches the Genesis account which states: "Then the Lord saw that the wickedness of man was great in the earth, and that every intent of the thoughts of his heart was only evil continually" (Genesis 6:5). Thus, from the first book of the Old Testament through 2 Peter, one of the last books written in the New Testament, the Bible exhibits complete and perfect unity in its dealing with Noah and the Flood. [NOTE: It is not the purpose of this discussion to verify the veracity and truth of the global Flood of Noah. That has been done successfully elsewhere (see Thompson, 1999). The sole purpose of this discussion is to show that the various Bible writers agree with each other in their individual assessments and statements regarding Noah and the Flood.]

Sodom and Gomorrah

The names of the cities of Sodom and Gomorrah are synonymous with wickedness throughout the books of the Bible. Genesis explains that Abraham and Lot had been traveling together after leaving the city of Haran. Due to the multitude of cattle possessed by both men, their respective herdsmen began to quarrel. Not wanting any root of strife to spring up between them, Abraham asked Lot to choose what land he would take, and Abraham suggested that he would separate from Lot by moving to a different area. Lot looked to the plain of Jordan and saw that it was well-watered, so he "pitched his tent even as far as Sodom" (Genesis 13:12). In the text immediately following Lot's decision, the Bible says: "But the men of Sodom were exceedingly wicked and sinful against the Lord" (Genesis 13:13).

Sodom and its sister city Gomorrah were so sinful that the Lord decided to destroy the cities by sending fire and brimstone from heaven to consume them. In Genesis 19, the text explains that Lot showed hospitality to angels sent from God. Lot attempted to protect the angels from being abused by the men of Sodom. In turn, the angels helped Lot escape the city before God destroyed it. The text also records that Lot's wife disobeyed the commandment of God delivered by the angels when she looked back at the city. As punishment for her disobedience, she was turned into a pillar of salt (Genesis 19:26).

Throughout the 66 books of the Bible, the destruction of Sodom and Gomorrah is referenced as an example of God's hatred of sin and His righteous judgment. The city of Sodom is mentioned over 40 times. The large majority of these instances have to do with the destruction brought on the city due to the wickedness of its inhabitants. The prophet Isaiah, in prophesying about the destruction of Babylon, noted that the wicked city would "be as when God overthrew Sodom and Gomorrah" (13:19). In Jeremiah's prophecy against the nation of Edom, the prophet said: "'As in the overthrow of Sodom and Gomorrah and their neighbors,' says the Lord, 'No one shall remain there, nor shall a son of man dwell in it'" (Jeremiah 49:18). Jeremiah also stated: "The punishment of the iniquity of the daughter of my people is greater than the punishment of the sin of Sodom, which was overthrown in a moment, with no hand to help her!" (Lamentations 4:6). Ezekiel mentioned that Sodom was proud and committed abominations in the sight of the Lord, therefore the Lord took the city away as He saw fit (16:50). Amos also referenced the destruction of Sodom and Gomorrah and associated it with fire and burning (4:11).

New Testament books present the same gruesome picture of wickedness and destruction as their Old Testament predecessors. In his gospel account, Luke recorded the words of Jesus, saying: "Likewise as it was also in the days of **Lot**: They ate, they drank, they bought, they sold, they planted, they built; but on the day that **Lot** went out of **Sodom** it rained **fire** and **brimstone** from heaven and destroyed them all" (17:28-29, emp. added). Notice the similarities between the statement made by Jesus and the Old Testament narrative. First, Lot was associated with the city of Sodom. Second, the city was destroyed on "the day" that Lot left, as the Genesis accounts asserts. Third, the destruction was caused by fire and brimstone sent from heaven (cf. Genesis 19:24). Additionally, in Luke 17:31-32, when Jesus admonished His listeners not to look back when they fled Jerusalem, He said: "Remember Lot's wife." He was obviously referring to the fact that she was turned to a pillar of salt when she looked back at Sodom.

The apostle Peter noted that God destroyed Sodom and Gomorrah, turning them to ashes, but saved righteous Lot who was oppressed by the filthy conduct of the Sodomites (2 Peter 2:6-8; cf. Jude 7). Lot's righteousness is referenced by Peter and seen in the Genesis account when he confronted the wicked men of Sodom who were bent on abusing the visiting angels. Lot went out to the Sodomites and said: "Please, my brethren, do not do so wickedly" (Genesis 19:7). Also, the apostle John makes a passing reference to the wickedness of Sodom in Revelation 11:8. Thus, from the first book of the Old Testament to the last book of the New Testament, we have a completely unified picture of the destruction of the cities of Sodom and Gomorrah based on their wickedness.

In truth, the narratives of Noah's Flood and the destruction of Sodom and Gomorrah are only two of literally hundreds of examples that could be produced to prove the Bible's unity. Stories about Moses, Abraham, Adam and Eve, Cain and Abel, Jacob and Esau, Joseph, Daniel, and Jonah provide equally impressive illustrations of the Bible's perfect cohesion.

MORAL UNITY OF THE BIBLE

The books of the Bible contain various moral themes that are treated consistently throughout the entire 66-book canon. A list of all such themes would exhaust the reader's patience, and would require a document comparable in length to the Bible itself. A brief sample, however, of these moral issues proves interesting and valuable to the overall discussion of the Bible's unity.

Lying

Throughout the Bible, the writers consistently present lying in a negative light, describing it as sin. In John 8:44, Jesus is quoted as saying that the devil "does not stand in the truth, because there is no truth in him. When he speaks a lie, he speaks from his own resources, for he is a liar, and the father of it." Jesus' statement about the devil is corroborated by the book of Genesis, in which the devil deceived Eve into thinking that she would escape death even if she disobeyed God and ate from the forbidden tree (Genesis 3:1-5,13). The apostle Paul also attested to Eve's deception in 1 Timothy 2:14–"And Adam was not deceived, but the woman being deceived, fell into transgression."

From the first chapters of Genesis, in which the devil's first lie is recorded, to the last book of Revelation, lying is condemned wholesale. Moses scaled Mount Sinai and received the Ten Commandments from God, the ninth of which was, "You shall not bear false witness against your neighbor" (Deuteronomy 5:20), or in other words, "you shall not lie about your neighbor." The psalmist wrote: "I hate and abhor lying, but I love your law" (Psalm 119:163). Solomon, the wisest man alive during his time, wrote: "These six things the Lord hates...a lying tongue...a false witness who speaks lies" (Proverbs 6:16-19). The Old Testament prophets wrote similar statements about lying: "Now go, write it before them on a tablet...that this is a rebellious people, lying children, children who will not hear the law of the Lord" (Isaiah 30:8-9).

The New Testament continues the thought of the Old Testament in its denunciation of lying. On one occasion, a rich young man came to Jesus, asking Him what was necessary to inherit eternal life. Jesus responded by telling him to keep the commandments. The young man then asked Jesus which commandments he needed to keep. Jesus said: "Do not commit adultery, do not murder, do not steal, **do not bear false witness**, do not defraud, honor your father and mother" (Mark 10:19, emp. added). In speaking of lying, it has already been noted that Jesus attributed such activity to the devil, and condemned it as a practice that is totally foreign to the character of God (John 8:44).

Luke, the writer of the book of Acts, recorded the story of Ananias and Sapphira, in which God struck dead a man and his wife for lying (Acts 5:1-11). The apostle Paul, in his letter to the young preacher Titus, noted that God cannot lie (Titus 1:2). Paul also wrote to the Christians in Ephesus: "Therefore, putting away lying, each one speak truth with his neighbor, for we are members of one another" (Ephesians 4:25). In Revelation, the last book of the New Testament, John wrote: "But the cowardly, unbelieving, abominable, murderers, sexually immoral, sorcerers, idolaters, and **all liars** shall have their part in the lake which burns with fire and brimstone, which is the second death" (Revelation 21:8).

Without fail, every Bible writer who comments on the moral value of lying condemns the practice. This fact, at first, may not seem remarkable, since many assume that lying has been condemned by every culture throughout history. But such is not the case. Under certain circumstances, a host of philosophers and teachers of morality have proposed that lying could be morally acceptable under certain circumstances. The atheistic writer Dan Barker is on record as saying: "We all know that it is sometimes necessary to tell a lie in order to protect someone from harm" (1992, p. 345, emp. added). Barker then illustrates with a scenario about a woman who is being hunted by her abusive husband, and he concluded: "I would consider it a **moral act** to lie to the man." Yet, it is not only atheistic thinkers like Barker who have suggested that lying could be moral. The esteemed early church writers Origen and John Chrysostom both believed and wrote that under certain conditions, lying could be morally acceptable. And the Greek philosopher Plato took a similar stance (see Slater, 2007).

But the Bible states that lying is always morally wrong, never morally permissible. Throughout the 1,600 years of its production, the books of the Bible consistently maintain the idea that lying is immoral. The practice is never justified by any of the 40 different writers. Although skeptics have alleged that the Bible condones lying under certain circumstances, such allegations have been proven to be baseless and false (see Thompson and Estabrook, 2004). Not a single

Bible writer swayed even a fraction in the unanimous condemnation of lying as a moral evil.

Additional examples of the moral unity of the Bible could easily be cited, including the Bible's condemnation of adultery, the command to honor one's parents, the prohibition on stealing and a host of others. [NOTE: The skeptic sometimes argues that since the Old Testament Law is no longer in force and the New Testament regulations differ from the Old, then God's moral code changed as well. However, this allegation is false. By altering the system of animal sacrifices and physical ordinances in the Old Testament, God's morality did not alter. For example, if the rules of baseball changed so that a person gets four strikes instead of three, that would not mean that the person could cheat by using a weighted bat. Changes in regulations are not equivalent to changes in moral judgments.]

DOCTRINAL UNITY OF THE NEW TESTAMENT

Elder Qualifications

Literally thousands of instances of internal agreement between the New Testament books could be listed. One such example involves the subtle mention of Peter as an elder. In 1 Peter 5:1, the text says: "The elders who are among you I exhort, **I who am a fellow elder** and a witness of the sufferings of Christ, and also a partaker of the glory that will be revealed" (emp. added). Of interest is the fact that, to be an elder, a man must be the "husband of one wife," as stated by Paul in his letter to Titus (1:6). From reading Luke's account of Jesus' life, we discover that on one occasion Jesus visited

Simon Peter's house, at which time He healed Peter's "wife's mother" of a high fever (4:38). Thus, we know that Peter was married and would meet the requirement to become an elder by being the husband of one wife. Of further interest is the fact that the apostle Paul, although he provided immense teaching and edification to the church, is never described as holding the office of elder in the church. The context of 1 Corinthians 11 indicates that Paul remained unmarried so that he could focus his attention on his ministry. Thus, Paul would not have been the husband of one wife, and would not have been qualified to be an elder. When these facts are synthesized, then, we can understand that subtle statements in the books of 1 Peter, Titus, Luke, and 1 Corinthians intertwine perfectly to give a consistent picture of the qualifications of an elder as they related to the lives of Peter and Paul.

The Lord's Supper

The examples and instructions pertaining to the Lord's Supper provide another clear instance of New Testament unity. Near the end of all four gospel accounts, Jesus and the 12 apostles gathered in an upper room to eat the Passover. During that feast, Jesus instituted what is commonly known today as the Lord's Supper. Luke's account of the event states: "And He took bread, gave thanks and broke it, and gave it to them, saying, 'This is My body which is given for you; do this in remembrance of Me.' Likewise He also took the cup after supper, saying, 'This cup is the new covenant in My blood, which is shed for you'" (22:19-20). The Lord's Supper, also known as communion (1 Corinthians

10:16), has been eaten in the assemblies of the church since its establishment.

Interestingly, the apostle Paul was not present with the Lord and the other apostles that night. In fact, during that time, his name was still Saul, and he was an unconverted Jewish leader. Yet, several years after his conversion, in his first letter to the Corinthians, Paul wrote:

> For I received from the Lord that which I also delivered to you: that the Lord Jesus on the **same night in which He was betrayed** took bread; and when He had given thanks, He broke it and said, "Take, eat; this is My body which is for you; do **this in remembrance of Me**." In the same manner He also took the cup after supper, saying, "**This cup is the new covenant in My blood**. This do, as often as you drink it, in remembrance of Me." For as often as you eat this bread and drink this cup, you proclaim the Lord's death till He comes (1 Corinthians 11:23-26, emp. added).

Notice how similar Paul's wording is to Jesus' statements in Luke. Both Luke and Paul acknowledge that this took place the night of Christ's betrayal. Paul then quotes Jesus verbatim in several lines, in complete accord with the accounts recorded in the Gospel.

Where does Paul claim to have gotten the information regarding the Lord's Supper? He explained to the Corinthians that he had received it "from the Lord" (1 Corinthians 11:23). But if Paul was not in the upper room the night of the betrayal, how would he have received such information "from the Lord"? In the first chapter of Paul's epistle to the Galatians, he is forced to defend his apostleship. In that context, he wrote to the Galatians: "But I make known to you, brethren, that the gospel which was preached by me is not according to man. For I neither received it from man, nor was I taught it, but it came through the revelation of Jesus Christ" (Galatians 1:11-12). Thus, Paul's statement that he had received the information concerning the Lord's Supper from Jesus would be consistent with the direct communication with Christ he claims to have had when writing to the Galatians. [NOTE: I am not, here, trying to defend Paul's claim of inspiration and direct revelation from Christ. The external evidences for the Bible's inspiration are explored further in other chapters of this book. Paul's statements in this connection are being used solely to show the unity and internal consistency in the New Testament writings.]

In addition to the remarkable consistency and similarity of Paul's statements in 1 Corinthians 11 concerning the Lord's Supper and those in the gospel accounts, other information regarding the communion confirms the unity of the New Testament documents. The gospel accounts make it clear that Jesus rose "on the first day of the week" (cf. John 20:1; Luke 24:1; Mark 16:2; Matthew 28:1). In 1 Corinthians 11, in the context of the Lord's Supper, Paul explains that the Corinthians were "coming together" to take the Lord's Supper. His statements indicate that the church at Corinth was eating the Lord's Supper during their worship assembly. Five chapters later, when Paul gave instructions for the monetary collection of the church, he wrote: "On the first day of the week let each one of you lay something aside, storing up as he may prosper, that there be no collections when I come" (1 Corinthians 16:2). This verse indicates that the Corinthian church met on the first day of the week, at which time they would have eaten the Lord's Supper and taken up their monetary contribution.

In Acts 20:7, the text states: "Now on the first day of the week, when the disciples came together to break bread, Paul, ready to depart the next day, spoke to them...." The phrase "to break bread" is used here to refer to the Lord's Supper (see Lyons, 2005b). Thus, the Bible provides an example of the church taking the Lord's Supper on the first day of the week and the Corinthian church meeting on the first day of the week to take up their collection and eat the Lord's Supper. The first day of the week was the New Testament day of meeting based on the historical fact that Jesus rose on that day. Such internal consistency between Luke, Acts, and 1 Corinthians testifies to the New Testament's inspiration.

Baptism

Throughout the New Testament, various Bible writers address the theme of baptism with remarkable consistency. Such consistency is even more impressive in light of the varied and contradictory opinions held by many today in the religious world about the subject.

After Jesus' resurrection, just before His ascension, He called His disciples together and issued to them what is often called the Great Commission. He said: "All authority has been given to Me in heaven and on earth. Go therefore and make disciples of all the nations, baptizing them in the name of the Father and of the Son and of the Holy Spirit, teaching them to observe all things that I have commanded you" (Matthew 28:18-20). From His instructions, it is clear that baptism plays a key role in the conversion of the lost. In fact, in Mark's account of the Gospel, he quotes Jesus as saying: "Go into all the world and preach the gospel to every creature. He who believes and is baptized will be saved; but he who does not believe will be condemned" (Mark 16:15-16). Mark's account of Jesus' statement clarifies the role of baptism, showing that it is an essential step in the salvation process.

The book of Acts records the history of the disciples fulfilling the Great Commission given to them by Christ. In Acts 2, we have the first recorded gospel sermon preached by Peter to the Jews in Jerusalem. In his powerful sermon, Peter explained to the Jews that they had crucified Jesus, the Messiah and Son of God. Many of the hearers believed Peter and asked what they needed to do. Peter responded by saying: "Repent, and let every one of you be baptized in the name of Jesus Christ for the remission of sins" (Acts 2:38). Notice that Peter connected baptism with the remission of sins, completely consistent with Jesus' statement in Mark requiring baptism for salvation. Throughout the book of Acts, water baptism is presented as a necessary step in the conversion of the lost to Christ (Acts 8:37-38; 9:18; 10:48; 16:15,31-33; 19:5). In fact, when the apostle Paul recounted his conversion, he quoted Ananias' statement to him as follows: "And now why are you waiting? Arise and be baptized, and wash away your sins, calling on the name of the Lord" (Acts 22:16). Here, again, baptism is connected with the washing away or forgiveness of sins.

In the epistles, baptism is consistently presented in a way that conforms perfectly to the gospel accounts and Acts. In his letter to the Romans, Paul stated:

> Or do you not know that as many of us as were baptized into Christ Jesus were baptized into His death? Therefore we were buried with Him through baptism into death, that just as Christ was raised from the dead by the glory of the Father, even so we also should walk in newness of life. For if we have been united together in the likeness of His death, certainly we also shall be in the likeness of His resurrection (Romans 6:3-5).

In these verses, Paul states that a person is baptized into Christ (cf. Galatians 3:27). In 2 Timothy 2:10, Paul says that salvation is in Christ. Thus, to obtain the salvation that is in Christ one must be baptized into Christ. Also note that Paul says that a person is baptized into the death of Christ (cf. Colossians 2:12). In Ephesians 1:7, Paul stated that the blood of Christ is the spiritual force that forgives a person's sins. That blood was shed at His death. Thus, when a person is baptized into Christ's death, he or she contacts the blood of Christ, linking baptism with the forgiveness of sins exactly as is presented in Acts 2:38, Acts 22:16, and as is implied in Mark 16:15-16.

The apostle Peter also spoke on baptism in a way that coincides flawlessly with Paul, Luke, Matthew, and Mark. Peter said: "There is also an antitype which now saves us—baptism (not the removal of the filth of the flesh, but the answer of a good conscience toward God), through the resurrection of Jesus Christ" (1 Peter 3:21). Notice that Peter connects baptism to salvation as the other writers, dependent upon the resurrection of Christ, exactly as Paul did. The New Testament's presentation of baptism provides an outstanding illustration of the unity of the New Testament books. [NOTE: Skeptics often have accused the Bible of being contradictory on certain points regarding the doctrine of baptism. For a refutation of such an idea see Lyons, 2005a, pp. 193-198.]

OBJECTIONS

The Writers Copied Each Other

The skeptic may attempt to suggest that much of the agreement and unity found in the Bible is unremarkable because the writers could have copied the information from books that were written prior to their own writings. Let us critically consider such an objection. First, the mere objection assumes the perfect unity of the 66 books of the Bible. Why would a skeptic be forced to suggest that the various writers copied each other if their unity and agreement could be disputed? The fact that the skeptic must resort to this charge is evidence of the reality of the Bible's unity.

Second, this allegation assumes that the various Old Testament prophets and New Testament writers had access to perfectly preserved texts of the various books they were "copying." Interestingly, skeptics often deny the accurate and complete transmission of the text. If a skeptic demands that the unity is a result of copying, he will be forced to admit the astonishing preservation of the text of the Bible. And, while the Christian gladly acknowledges that such preservation did occur, and that some material would naturally be based on previous texts, it is not the case that the various writers would have had ready access to all the texts before they wrote.

Furthermore, non-canonical writers who had many of the same texts preserved for them wrote material that contradicted the canonical Scriptures. How is it that not a single book in the 66-book canon contains a single legitimate contradiction? Even if every writer had a copy of every other book in front of him before he wrote, such unity would be impossible from a human standpoint. In truth, individuals often contradict their own writings due to a slip of the mind or a change in their previous thinking. Yet no such slips, changes, or other aberrant occurrences can be found in the 66-book library of the Bible.

The Bible Contains Contradictions

Skeptics often suggest that the unity of the Bible is only superficial. They say that even though it might look like it is unified in its themes, on closer inspection it contains hundreds of discrepancies and contradictions. Dennis McKinsey, the author of *The Skeptics Annotated Bible,* stated:

> Every analyst of the Bible should realize that the Book is a veritable miasma of contradictions, inconsistencies, inaccuracies, poor science, bad math, inaccurate geography, immoralities, degenerate heroes, false prophecies, boring repetitions, childish superstitions, silly miracles, and dry-as-dust discourse. **But contradictions remain the most obvious, the most potent, the most easily proven, and the most common problem to plague the Book** (1995, p. 71, emp. added).

Yet, McKinsey and others have no legitimate basis to support the accusation that the Bible contradicts itself. Christian apologist Eric Lyons has done extensive work on the subject of alleged Bible contradictions, in which he has successfully refuted the idea that the various books of the Bible contradict each other. He has written two volumes of *The Anvil Rings* that provide over 500 pages of material refuting specific accusations made by the skeptic (2003; 2005a). In fact, for the last 2,000 years, a long line of competent Christian apologists have thoroughly and effectively refuted the charges of alleged biblical discrepancies (e.g., Gaussen, 1850; Haley, 1876; et al.). Even a cursory look at such research forces the honest student to conclude that **if** the Bible does, in fact, contain a genuine contradiction of some kind, it **has not yet been found.** When all the facts are considered, each alleged biblical contradiction has been shown to be something other than a legitimate contradiction. That is a powerful statement, considering the fact that no book in the world has been examined more closely or scrutinized more carefully. After the Bible has been put under the high-powered microscope of hostile criticism, and dissected by the razor-sharp scalpel of supposed contradictions, it rises from the surgery with no scratches or scars, none the worse for wear.

CONCLUSION

No series of books in human history has maintained the supernatural internal consistency that is present within the pages of the Bible. From the first book of Genesis to the last book of Revelation, approximately

40 men penned individual treatises that combine to form the best-selling, most widely distributed, perfectly unified, flawlessly written book ever produced. Mere human genius could never have accomplished such an extraordinary feat. As the psalmist aptly spoke of God's Word 3,000 years ago: "The entirety of Your word is truth, and every one of Your righteous judgments endures forever" (Psalm 119:160).

CHAPTER 5

FACTUAL ACCURACY OF THE OLD TESTAMENT

A man with a leather vest and a broad-rimmed hat wraps a torn piece of cloth around an old bone, sets it on fire, and uses it as a torch to see his way through ancient tunnels filled with bones, rats, bugs, and buried treasure. Close behind him lurks the dastardly villain ready to pounce on the treasure after the hero has done all the planning and dangerous work. We have seen this scenario, and others very similar to it, time and again in movies like *Indiana Jones* or *The Mummy*. And although we understand that Hollywood exaggerates and dramatizes the situation, it still remains a fact that finding ancient artifacts excites both young and old alike. Finding things left by people of the past is exciting because a little window into their lives is opened to us. When we find an arrowhead, we learn that the Indians used bows and arrows to hunt and fight. Discovering a piece of pottery tells us how the ancients cooked or drew water from wells. Every tiny artifact gives the modern person a more complete view of life in the past.

Because of the value of archaeology, many have turned to it in order to answer certain questions about the past. One of the questions most often asked is, "Did the things recorded in the Bible really happen?" Truth be told, archaeology cannot always answer that question. Nothing material remains from Elijah's trip in the fiery chariot, and no physical artifacts exist to show that Christ actually walked on water. Therefore, if we ask archaeology to "prove" that the entire Bible is true or false, we are faced with the fact that archaeology can neither prove nor disprove the Bible's validity. However, even though it cannot conclusively prove the Bible's validity, archaeology does provide important pieces of the past that consistently verify the Bible's historical and factual accuracy. This chapter is designed to bring to light a small fraction of the significant archaeological finds that have been instrumental in corroborating the biblical text of the Old Testament.

HEZEKIAH AND SENNACHERIB

When King Hezekiah assumed the throne in Judah, he did so under the most distressed conditions. His father, Ahaz, had turned to the gods of Damascus, cut in pieces the articles of the house of God, and shut the doors of the temple of the Lord. In addition, he had made high places "in every single city" where he sacrificed and offered incense to other gods (2 Chronicles 28:22-27). The people of Judah followed Ahaz, and the Bible says: "The Lord brought Judah low because of Ahaz king of Israel, for he had encouraged moral decline in Judah and had been continually unfaithful to the Lord" (2 Chronicles 28:19).

Upon this troubled throne, King Hezekiah began to rule at the youthful age of 25. He reigned for 29 years, and the inspired text declares that he "did what was right in the sight of the Lord, according to all that his father David had done" (2 Chronicles 29:2). Among other reforms, Hezekiah reopened the temple, reestablished the observance of the Passover, and appointed the priests to receive tithes and administer their proper duties in the temple. After completing these reforms, Scripture states that "Sennacherib king of Assyria entered Judah; he encamped against the fortified cities, thinking to win them over to himself" (2 Chronicles 32:1).

It is here that we turn to the secular record of history to discover that the powerful nation Assyria, under the reign of King Sargon II, had subdued many regions in and around Palestine. Upon Sargon's death, revolt broke out within the Assyrian empire. Sennacherib, the new Assyrian monarch, was determined to maintain a firm grasp on his vassal states, which would mean that he would be forced to invade the cities of Judah if Hezekiah continued to defy Assyria's might (Hoerth, 1998, pp. 341-352). Knowing that Sennacherib would not sit idly by and watch his empire crumble, King Hezekiah began to make preparations for the upcoming invasion. One of the preparations he made was to stop the water from the springs that ran outside of Jerusalem and to redirect the water into the city by way of a tunnel. Second Kings 20:20 records the construction of the tunnel in these words: "Now the rest of the acts of Hezekiah–all his might, and how he made a pool and a tunnel and brought water into the city–are they not written in the book of chronicles of the kings of Judah?" The biblical text from 2 Chronicles 32:30 further substantiates the tunnel construction with this recorded statement: "This same Hezekiah also stopped the water outlet of Upper Gihon, and brought the water by tunnel to the west side of the City of David." The tunnel, today known as "Hezekiah's tunnel," stands as one of the paramount archaeological attestations to the biblical text. Carved through solid limestone, the tunnel meanders in an S-shape under the city of Jerusalem for a length of approximately 1,800 feet. In 1880, two young boys swimming at the site rediscovered an inscription about 20 feet from the exit that detailed how the tunnel was made:

> ...And this was the account of the breakthrough. While the laborers were still working with their picks, each toward the other, and while there were still three cubits to be broken through, the voice of each was heard calling to the other, because there was a crack (or split or overlap) in the rock from the south to the north. And at the moment of the breakthrough, the laborers struck each toward the other, pick against pick. Then water flowed from the spring to the pool for 1,200 cubits. And the height of the rock above the heads of the laborers was 100 cubits (Price, 1997, p. 267).

Of the inscription, John C.H. Laughlin wrote that it is "one of the most important, as well as famous, inscriptions ever found in Judah" (2000, p. 145). Incidentally, since the length of the tunnel was about 1,800 feet and the inscription marked the tunnel at "1,200 cubits," archaeologists have a good indication that the cubit was about one and a half feet at the time of Hezekiah (Free and Vos, 1992, p. 182).

Hezekiah dug his tunnel in order to keep a steady supply of water pumping into Jerusalem during the anticipated siege of Sennacherib. Today it stands as a strong witness to the accuracy of the biblical historical record of 2 Kings and 2 Chronicles.

In addition to Hezekiah's tunnel, other amazingly detailed archaeological evidence gives us an outstanding record of events between Hezekiah and Sennacherib as they unfolded. Much of the information we have comes from the Taylor Prism. This six-sided clay artifact stands about 15 inches tall and was found in Nineveh in 1830 by the British Colonel R. Taylor. Thus, it is known as the "Taylor Prism" (Price, 1997, pp. 272-273). The prism contains six columns covered by over 500 lines of writing. It was purchased in the Winter of 1919-1920 by J.H. Breasted for the Oriental Institute in Chicago (Hanson, 2002).

Part of the text on the Taylor Prism has Sennacherib's account of what happened in his military tour of Judah:

> As to Hezekiah, the Jew, he did not submit to my yoke, I laid siege to 46 of his strong cities, walled forts and to the countless small villages in their vicinity, and conquered (them) by means of well-stamped (earth-)ramps, and battering-rams brought (thus) near (to the walls) (combined with) the attack by foot soldiers, (using) mines, breeches as well as sapper work. I drove out (of them) 200,150 people, young and old, male and female, horses, mules, donkeys, camels, big and small cattle beyond counting, and considered (them) booty. Himself I made a prisoner in Jerusalem, his royal residence, like a bird in a cage. I surrounded him with earthwork in order to molest those who were leaving his city's gate (Pritchard, 1958a, p. 200).

At least two facts of monumental significance reside in Sennacherib's statement. First, Sennacherib's attack on the outlying cities of Judah finds a direct parallel in 2 Chronicles 32:1: "Sennacherib king of Assyria came and entered Judah; he encamped against the fortified cities...." The most noteworthy fortified city besieged and captured by the Assyrian despot was the city of Lachish. Second, Sennacherib never mentions that he captured the city of Jerusalem.

Lachish Under Seige

When we turn to the biblical account of Sennacherib's Palestinian invasion in 2 Kings 18, we read that he had advanced against "all the fortified cities of Judah" (vs. 14). At one of those cities, Lachish, King Hezekiah sent tribute money in an attempt to assuage the Assyrian's wrath. The text states: "Then Hezekiah king of Judah sent to the king of Assyria at Lachish, saying, 'I have done wrong; turn away from me; whatever you impose on me I will pay'" (vs. 14). From Lachish, Sennacherib demanded 300 talents of silver and 30 talents of gold, which Hezekiah promptly paid. Not satisfied, however, the Assyrian ruler "sent the Tartan, the Rabsaris, and the Rabshakeh from Lachish, with a great army against Jerusalem, to King Hezekiah" (vs. 17) in an attempt to frighten the denizens of Jerusalem into surrender. The effort failed, "so the Rabshakeh returned and found the king of Assyria warring against Libnah, for he heard that he had departed from Lachish" (19:8). From the biblical record, then, we discover very scant information about the battle at Lachish–only that Sennacherib was there, laid siege to the city (2

Chronicles 32:9) and moved on to Libnah upon the completion of his siege.

From Sennacherib's historical files, however, we get a much more complete account of the events surrounding Lachish. The Assyrian monarch considered his victory at Lachish of such import that he dedicated an entire wall (nearly 70 linear feet) of his palace in Nineveh to carved wall reliefs depicting the event (Hoerth, 1998, p. 350). In the mid 1840s, the famous English archaeologist Henry Layard began extensive excavations in the ruins of ancient Nineveh. He published his initial findings in a best-selling volume titled *Nineveh and its Remains* (1849), and subsequent volumes titled *The Monuments of Nineveh* (1849); *Inscriptions in the Cuneiform Characters* (1851); and *Discoveries in the Ruins of Nineveh* (1853) [see Moorey, 1991, pp. 7-12 for more about Layard's work]. Since Layard's early discoveries, archaeologists have located and identified thousands of artifacts from at least three different palaces. The remains of ancient Nineveh are located in two mounds on opposite banks of the Hawsar River. One mound, known as Kouyunjik Tepe, contained the remains of the palaces of Esarhaddon and Ashurbanipal. The other mound, Nebi Younis, held the relics of the palace of Sennacherib. These palaces were built on raised platforms about 75 feet high (Negev and Gibson, 2001, p. 369).

One of the most outstanding artifacts found among the ruins of Nineveh was the wall relief depicting Sennacherib's defeat of the walled city of Lachish. Ephraim Stern offers an excellent description of the events pictured in the relief:

> The main scene shows the attack on the gate wall
> of Lachish. The protruding city gate is presented

in minute detail, with its crenellations and its
special reinforcement by a superstructure of war-
riors' shields. The battering rams were moved over
specially constructed ramps covered with wooden
logs. They were "prefabricated," four-wheeled, tur-
reted machines. The scene vividly shows frenzied
fighting of both attacker and defender in the final
stage of battle (2001, 2:5).

Stern also mentions flaming firebrands that the defend-
ers of Lachish launched at its attackers, long-handled,
ladle-like instruments used to dowse the front of the
battering rams when they were set on fire, slingman,
archers, and assault troops with spears. One of the
most striking features of the relief is the depiction of
the tortures inflicted on the inhabitants of Lachish.
Several prisoners are pictured impaled on poles while
women and children from the city are led past the
victims (2:5-6). The epigraph that accompanied the
relief read: "Sennacherib, king of the world, king of
Assyria, sat upon a *nimedu*-throne and passed in review
the booty (taken) from Lachish (*La-ki-su*) (Pritchard,
1958a, p. 201).

Of further interest is the fact that archaeological digs at the city of Lachish bear out the details of
Sennacherib's wall relief. Extensive archaeological digs
at Lachish in 1935-1938 by the British, and again in
1973-1987 under Israeli archaeologists, David Ussishkin
and others, have revealed a treasure trove of artifacts
that fit the events depicted by Sennacherib. Concerning
the Assyrian siege of Lachish, Dever noted:

The evidence of it is all there: the enormous slop-
ing siege ramp thrown up against the city walls
south of the gate; the double line of defense walls,

upslope and downslope; the iron-shod Assyrian battering rams that breached the city wall at its highest point; the massive destruction within the fallen city.... Virtually all the details of the Assyrian reliefs have been confirmed by archaeology.... Also brought to light by the excavators were the double city walls; the complex siege ramp, embedded with hundreds of iron arrowheads and stone ballistae; the counter-ramp inside the city; the destroyed gate, covered by up to 6 ft. of destruction debris; huge boulders from the city wall, burned almost to lime and fallen far down the slope... (2001, pp. 168-169).

Indeed, the Assyrian monarch's seige of Lachish is documented by the biblical text, and the destruction of the city is corroborated by the massive carving dedicated to the event in Sennacherib's palace at Nineveh, as well as the actual artifacts found in stratum III at Lachish.

Jerusalem Stands Strong

Of special interest in Sennacherib's description of his Palestinian conquest is the fact that he never mentioned taking the city of Jerusalem. On the Taylor Prism, we find the writings about his conquest of 46 outlying cities, in addition to "walled forts" and "countless small villages." In fact, we even read that Hezekiah was shut up in Jerusalem as a prisoner "like a bird in a cage." It is also recorded that Hezekiah sent more tribute to Sennacherib at the end of the campaign (Pritchard, 1958a, pp. 200-201). What is not recorded, however, is any list of booty that was taken from the capital city of Judah. Nor is an inventory of prisoners given in the text of the Taylor Prism. Indeed, one would think that if the city of Lachish deserved so much attention from the Assyrian dictator, then the capital city of Judah would deserve even more.

What we find, however, is complete silence as to the capturing of the city. What happened to the vast, conquering army to cause it to buckle at the very point of total victory? Hershel Shanks, of *Biblical Archaeology Review*, wrote, "...although we don't know for sure what broke the siege, we do know that the Israelites managed to hold out" (1995, p. 84).

The biblical text, however, offers the answer to this historical enigma. Due to Hezekiah's faithfulness to the Lord, Jehovah offered His assistance to the Judean King. In the book of Isaiah, the prophet was sent to Hezekiah with a message of hope. Isaiah informed Hezekiah that God would stop Sennacherib from entering the city, because Hezekiah prayed to the Lord for assistance. In Isaiah 37:36, the text states:

> Then the angel of the Lord went out, and killed in the camp of the Assyrians one hundred and eighty-five thousand; and when people arose early in the morning, there were the corpses–all dead. So Sennacherib king of Assyria departed and went away, returned home, and remained at Nineveh.

Sennacherib could not boast of his victory over the city of Jerusalem, because there was no victory. The Lord delivered the city out of his hand. In addition, Dever noted: "Finally, Assyrian records note that Sennacharib did die subsequently at the hands of assassins, his own sons..." (2001, p. 171). Luckenbill records the actual inscription from Esarhaddon's chronicles that describe the event:

In the month Nisanu, on a favorable day, comply-
ing with their exalted command, I made my joyful
entrance into the royal palace, an awesome place,
wherein abides the fate of kings. A firm determination fell upon my brothers. They forsook the gods
and turned to their deeds of violence plotting evil....
To gain the kingship they slew Sennacherib, their
father (1989, 2:200-201).

These events and artifacts surrounding Hezekiah,
Sennacherib, Lachish, and Jerusalem give us an amazing glimpse into the tumultuous relationship between
Judah and her neighbors. These facts also provide an
excellent example of how archaeology substantiates
the biblical account.

THE SIGNIFICANCE OF BULLAE

The ancient Israelites used several different mediums to record information. Among the most popular
was the use of papyrus and leather scrolls. When an
ancient scribe completed writing his information on
a scroll, he would often roll the papyrus or leather
into a cylinder shape and tie it securely with a string.
In order to seal the string even more securely, and to
denote the author or sender of the scroll, a soft bead of
clay was placed over the string of the scroll. With some
type of stamping device, the clay was pressed firmly
to the scroll, leaving an inscription in the clay (King
and Stager, 2001, p. 307). These clay seals are known
as bullae (which is the plural form of the word bulla).
Over the many years of archaeological excavations,
many hundreds of these bullae have been discovered.
The *Archaeological Encyclopedia of the Holy Land* gives an
extensive list of bullae that have been unearthed: In

Samaria during the 1930s, 50 were found, 17 at Lachish in 1966, 51 in Jerusalem in digs conducted by Y. Shiloh, 128 in 1962 found in the Wadi ed-Daliyeh Cave, and a large cache of 2,000 bullae found in 1998 at Tel Kadesh (Negev and Gibson, 2001, pp. 93-94).

Most of the bullae that have been discovered are small, oval, clay stamps that contain the name of the person responsible for the document that was sealed, and occasionally the father of that person, title or office of the sealer, and/or a picture of an animal or some other artistic rendering. One of the most interesting things about the bullae that have been discovered is the fact that certain names found among the clay seals correspond with biblical references. For instance, from 1978-1985, Yigal Shiloh did extensive digging in the city of Jerusalem. In 1982, in a building in Area G of Jerusalem, he discovered a cache of 51 bullae. Because of these clay inscriptions, the building is known in archaeological circles as the "House of Bullae." This building was burned during the Babylonian destruction of Jerusalem in 586 B.C. Unfortunately, the intense heat of the fires burned all the leather and papyrus scrolls. Yet, even though it destroyed the scrolls, the same fire baked the clay bullae hard and preserved them for posterity (King and Stager, 2001, p. 307). One of the names inscribed on a bulla was the Hebrew name "Gemaryahu [Gemariah] the son of Shaphan." Price noted: "This name, which appears a few times in the book of Jeremiah, was the name of the scribe who served in the court of King Jehoiakim" (1997, p. 235). Jeremiah 36:10 records that Jeremiah's scribe Baruch read from the words of the prophet "in the chamber of

Gemariah the son of Shaphan the scribe...." It is also interesting to note that Gemariah was a scribe, which would have put him in just the position to produce bullae. Also among the collection from the "House of Bullae" was a bulla sealed with the name "Azaryahu son of Hilqiyahu"—a name that easily corresponds with Azariah son of Hilkiah found in 1 Chronicles 9:10-11 (Laughlin, 2000, p. 153).

Another interesting bulla, and probably the most famous, is connected to the scribe of Jeremiah–Baruch. Hershal Shanks, writing for the journal of which he is the editor–*Biblical Archaeology Review*–gave a detailed account of a landmark cache of bullae. In October of 1975, the first four bullae of a hoard that would eventually tally over 250, were purchased by an antiquities dealer in east Jerusalem. The dealer took these bullae to Nahman Avigad, a leading Israeli expert on ancient seals at Hebrew University. More and more bullae came across Avigad's desk that fit with the others. On more than one occasion, a fragment from one collection would fit with a corresponding fragment from another dealer's collection. Ultimately, Yoav Sasson, a Jerusalem collector, came to acquire about 200 of the bullae, and Reuben Hecht obtained 49 pieces (1987, pp. 58-65).

The names on two of these bullae have captivated the archaeological world for several decades now. On one of the bulla, the name "Berekhyahu son of Neriyahu the scribe" is clearly impressed. Shanks wrote concerning this inscription: "The common suffix –*yahu* in ancient Hebrew names, especially in Judah, is a form of Yahweh. Baruch means "the blessed." Berekhyahu means "blessed of Yahweh." An equivalent form to –*yahu* is –*yah*, traditionally rendered as "-iah" in English translations. Neriah is really Neri-yah or Neriyahu. Eighty of the 132 names represented in the hoard (many names appear more than once on the 250 bullae) include the theophoric element –*yahu* (1987, p. 61). Shanks went on to conclude, along with the general consensus of archaeological scholars, that the bulla belonged to Baruch, the scribe of Jeremiah. In Jeremiah 36:4 the text reads: "Then Jeremiah called Baruch the son of Neriah...." The name on the bulla corresponds well with the name in Jeremiah. Concerning the bulla, Hoerth wrote: "This lump of clay...used to close a papyrus document, was sealed by none other than 'Baruch son of Neriah' (Jer. 36:4). Baruch's name here carries a suffix abbreviation for God, indicating that his full name meant 'blessed of God'" (1998, p. 364).

To multiply the evidence that this inscription was indeed the Baruch mentioned in Jeremiah, another of the inscriptions from a bulla in the cache documented the title "Yerahme'el son of the king." This name corresponds to King Jehoiakim's son "who was sent on the unsuccessful mission to arrest Baruch and Jeremiah" (Shanks, 1987, p. 61). Indeed, the biblical text states: "And the king commanded Jerahmeel the king's son... to seize Baruch the scribe and Jeremiah the prophet, but the Lord hid them" (Jeremiah 36:26). A. Mazar, among the most notable archaeologists, commenting on the bulla, said about Jerahmeel the king's son, "we presume [he–KB] was Jehoiakim's son sent to arrest Jeremiah (Jeremiah 36:26)" (1992, pp. 519-520). [NOTE: the Hebrew letters represented by Y and J often are used interchangeably in the English transliteration of Hebrew names; a fact that can be seen easily in the Hebrew name for God which is variously written Yahweh or Jehovah.] Another bulla in the hoard contained the title "Elishama, servant of the king." And in Jeremiah 36:12, the text noted one "Elishama the scribe." While Professor Avigad thinks it would be a dubious connection, since he believes the biblical text would not drop the title "servant of the king" because of its prestige, Shanks commented: "I would not reject the identification so easily" (1987, p. 62).

We have then, among this phenomenal cache of bullae, which date to the time of the events in the book of Jeremiah, two names and titles that correspond almost identically to Baruch the son of Neriah and Jerahmeel the son of Jehoiakim, and a third, Elishama, whose name at least appears in Jeremiah 36. What, then, does this prove? While it is the case that several men in ancient Israel could be named Baruch or Jerahmeel, it becomes almost absurd to suggest that these bullae just happen coincidentally to correspond to the biblical text so well. Such evidence points overwhelming to the accuracy of the biblical text and its historical verifiability. [As an added note of interest on the Baruch bulla, Shanks wrote a follow-up article in *Biblical Archaeological Review* in 1996 in which he discussed another bulla with Baruch's title on it that also contains a fingerprint–possibly of the scribe himself. This bulla is in the private collection of a well-known collector named Shlomo Maussaieff (Shanks, 1996, pp. 36-38).]

THE MOABITE STONE

Another important archaeological find verifying the historicity of the biblical account is known as the Moabite Stone. It is true that writing about a rock which was discovered almost 150 years ago certainly would not fit in a current "in the news" section. In fact, since 1868, so much has been written about this stone that very few new articles pertaining to it come to light. But the truth of the matter is that even though it was discovered more than a century ago, people need to be reminded of its importance.

The stone is known as the Moabite Stone, or the Mesha Inscription, since it was written by Mesha, the king of Moab. A missionary named F.A. Klein first discovered the stone in August of 1868 (Edersheim, n.d., 6:109). When he initially saw the black basalt stone, it measured approximately 3 1/2 feet high and 2 feet wide. Upon hearing of Klein's adventure, a French scholar named Clermont-Ganneau located the antiquated piece of rock and copied eight lines of the stone. He also had an impression, called a squeeze, made of the writing on its surface. A squeeze is made by placing a soggy piece of paper over the inscription, which retains the form of the inscription when dry (Pritchard, 1958b, p. 105). From that point, the details surrounding the stone are not quite as clear. Apparently, the Arabs who had the stone decided to shatter it for reasons unknown. [Some reasons given include the idea that they thought it was a religious talisman of some sort, or they thought they could get more money selling the stone in pieces. However, LeMaire claims that these reasons are "apocryphal" and says they broke it because they hated the

Ottomans who were attempting to purchase the stone (1994, p. 34).] By heating it in fire and then pouring cold water on it, they succeeded in breaking the stone into several pieces. The pieces were scattered, but about two-thirds of the original stone has been relocated and currently resides at the Louvre in Paris (Jacobs and McCurdy, 2002).

The written inscription on the stone provides a piece of outstanding evidence verifying the Bible's accuracy. Mesha, the king of Moab, had the stone cut *circa* 850 B.C. to tell of his many conquests and his reacquisition of certain territories that were controlled by Israel. In the 30-line text composed of about 260 words, Mesha mentions that Omri was the king of Israel who had oppressed Moab, but then Mesha says he "saw his desire upon" Omri's son and upon "his house." Mesha wrote:

> I (am) Mesha, son of Chemosh-[...], king of Moab, the Dibonite—my father (had) reigned over Moab thirty years, and I reigned after my father, –(who) made this high place for Chemosh in Qarhoh [...] because he saved me from all the kings and caused me to triumph over all my adversaries. As for Omri, (5) king of Israel, he humbled Moab many years (lit., days), for Chemosh was angry at his land. And his son followed him and he also said, "I will humble Moab." In my time he spoke (thus), but I have triumphed over him and over his house, while Israel hath perished forever (Pritchard, 1958a, p. 209).

The Mesha stele cites Omri as the king of Israel, just as 1 Kings 16:21-28 indicates. Furthermore, it mentions Omri's son (Ahab) in close connection with the Moabites, as does 2 Kings 3:4-6. In addition, both the stele and 2 Kings 3:4-6 list Mesha as the king of Moab. Later in the inscription, the stele further names the Israelite tribe of Gad, and the Israelite God, Yahweh. Not only are the references to the Israelite kings quite notable, but also Pritchard commented that this reference to Yahweh is one of the few that have been found outside Palestine proper (1958b, 106).

Another important feature of the Moabite stone is the fact that it "gave the solution to a question that had gone unanswered for centuries." Alfred Hoerth recounts how the biblical record chronicles the Moabite subjugation under king David and king Solomon, but that the Moabites broke free at the beginning of the divided kingdom. However, in the next biblical reference to Moab, 2 Kings 3:4, the Bible records that Ahab was receiving tribute from Moab. "Nowhere does the Bible state how or when Moab was reclaimed for Ahab to be receiving such tribute. The Moabite Stone provides that information, telling, as it does, of Omri's conquest from the Moabite point of view" (1998, p. 310).

From the end of the quoted portion of the Mesha Inscription ("while Israel hath perished forever"), it is obvious that Mesha exaggerated the efficacy of his conquest, a common practice among ancient kings. Pritchard noted that historians agree that "the Moabite chroniclers tended generally, and quite understandably, to ignore their own losses and setbacks" (1958b, p. 106). Free and Vos document the works of John D. Davies and S.L. Caiger, which offer a harmonization of the Moabite text with the biblical record. Davies, formerly of the Princeton Seminary, accurately observed: "Mesha is in no wise contradicting, but only unintentionally supplementing the Hebrew account" (1992, p. 161).

As a further point of interest, the French scholar André LeMaire, in an extensive article in *Biblical Ar chaeology Review,* has "identified the reading of the name *David* in a formerly unreadable line, 'House of D...,' on the Mesha Stele (or Moabite Stone)" (Price, 1997, p. 171; see also LeMaire, 1994, pp. 30-37). Whether or not this identification is accurate has yet to be verified completely by scholarly consensus. Even the liberal scholars Finkelstein and Silberman, however, noted LaMaire's identification along with the Tel Dan inscription documenting the House of David, and concluded: "Thus, the house of David was known throughout the region, this clearly validates the biblical description of a figure named David becoming the founder of the dynasty of Judahite kings in Jerusalem" (2001, p. 129).

Taken as a whole, the Moabite stone remains one of the most impressive pieces of evidence verifying the historical accuracy of the Old Testament. And, although this find has been around almost 150 years, it "still speaks" to us today (Hebrews 11:4).

THE CYRUS CYLINDER

Cyrus, the king of the Medo-Person Empire, stands among the more important foreign rulers of the Israelite nation. In fact, many Old Testament prophecies revolve around this monarch. The prophet Isaiah documented that the Babylonian Empire would fall to the Medes and the Persians (Isaiah 13; 21:1-10). Not only did Isaiah detail the particular empire to which the Babylonians would fall, but he also called Cyrus by name (Isaiah 44:28; 45:1-5). Amazingly, Isaiah's prophecy was made approximately 150 years before Cyrus was born (Isaiah prophesied in about 700 B.C., Cyrus took the city of Babylon in 539 B.C.). To add to Cyrus' significance, Isaiah predicted that Cyrus would act as the Lord's "shepherd." In fact, Isaiah recorded these words of the Lord concerning Cyrus: "And he shall perform all My pleasure, even saying to Jerusalem, 'You shall be built,' and to the temple, 'Your foundation shall be laid'" (Isaiah 44:28).

In 1879, Hormoz Rasam found a small clay cylinder (about nine inches long) in the ancient city of Babylon (now in the British Museum). Upon the clay cylinder, King Cyrus had inscribed, among other things, details of his victory over the city of Babylon and his policy toward the nations he had captured, as well as his policy toward their various gods and religions. Price records a translation of a segment of the cuneiform text found on the cylinder:

> ...I returned to [these] sacred cities on the other side of the Tigris, the sanctuaries of which have been in ruins for a long time, the images which [used] to live therin and established for them permanent sanctuaries. I [also] gathered all their [former] inhabitants and returned [to them] their habitations. Furthermore, I resettled upon the command of Marduk the great lord, all the gods of Sumer and Akkad whom Nabonidus has brought into Babylon to the anger of the lord of the gods, unharmed, in their [former] chapels, the places which made them happy. May all the gods who I have resettled in their sacred cities ask daily Bel and Nebo for long life for me and may they recommend me...to Marduk, my lord, may they say thus: Cyrus, the king who worships you and

> Cambyses, his son, [...] all of them I settled in a
> peaceful place (1997, pp. 251-252).

The policy, often hailed as Cyrus' declaration of human rights, coincides with the biblical account of the ruler's actions, in which Cyrus decreed that the temple in Jerusalem should be rebuilt and all the exiled Israelites who wished to join in the venture had his permission and blessing to do so (Ezra 1:1-11). The little nine-inch clay cylinder stands with the other archaeological evidences that corroborate, in minute detail, the historical accuracy of the biblical text.

CONCLUSION

The archaeological evidence presented in this chapter that confirms the biblical history is, in truth, only a tiny fraction of the evidence that could be amassed along these lines. Countless volumes of hundreds of pages have been produced to this point, and with every new find comes new information that will fill archaeological texts for decades to come. The more we uncover the past, the more we uncover the truth that the Bible is the most trustworthy, historically accurate document ever produced. As John Greenleaf Whittier once wrote:

> We search the world for truth; we cull the good, the
> pure, the beautiful, from all the old flower fields of
> the soul; and, weary seekers of the best, we come
> back laden from our quest, to find that all the sages
> said is in the Book our mothers read.

CHAPTER 6

FACTUAL ACCURACY OF THE NEW TESTAMENT

Any time a book alleges to report historical events accurately, that book opens itself up to an immense amount of criticism. If such a book claims to be free from all errors in its historical documentation, the criticism becomes even more intense. Such **should** be the case, for it is the responsibility of present and future generations to know and understand the past, and to insist that history, including certain monumental moments, is recorded and related as accurately as possible. The New Testament does not claim to be a systematic representation of first-century history. It is not, per se, merely a history book. It does, however, claim that the historical facts related in the text are accurate, without error (2 Timothy 3:16-17; Acts 1:1-3). Due to this extraordinary claim, the New Testament has been scrutinized more closely than any other text in existence (except maybe its companion, the Old Testament). What has been the result of such scrutiny? The overwhelming result of this intense examination is an enormous cache of amazing archaeological evidence that testifies to the exactitude of the historical references in the New Testament. As can be said of virtually every article on archaeology and the Bible, the following few pages that document this archaeological evidence only scratch the surface of the available evidence. Nevertheless, an examination of this subject makes for a fascinating study in biblical accuracy.

THE PILATE INSCRIPTION

Few who have read the New Testament accounts of the trial of Jesus can forget the name Pontius Pilate. All four gospel accounts make reference to Pilate. His inquisition of Jesus at the insistence of the Jewish mob stands as one of the most memorable scenes in the life of Jesus. No less than three times, this Roman official explained to the howling mob that he found no fault with Jesus (John 18:38; 19:4,6). Wanting to placate the Jews, however, Pilate washed his hands in a ceremonial attestation to his own innocence of the blood of Christ, and delivered Him to be scourged and crucified.

What can be gleaned from secular history concerning Pilate? For nearly 2000 years, the only references to Pilate were found in such writings as Josephus and Tacitus. The written record of his life placed him as the Roman ruler over Judea from A.D. 26-36. The records indicate that Pilate was a very rash, often violent man. The biblical record even mentioned that Pilate had killed certain Galileans while they were presenting sacrifices (Luke 13:1). Besides an occasional reference to Pilate in certain written records, however, there were no inscriptions or stone monuments that documented his life.

Such remained the case until 1961. In that year, Pilate moved from a figure known solely from ancient literature, to a figure attested to by archaeology. The Roman officials who controlled Judea during Jesus' time, most likely made their headquarters in the ancient town of Caesarea, as evinced from two references by Josephus to Pilate's military and political activity in that city (Finegan, 1992, p. 128). Located in Caesarea was a large Roman theater that an Italian-sponsored group of archaeologists began to excavate in 1959. Two years later, in 1961, researchers found a two-foot by three-foot slab of rock that had been used "in the construction of a landing between flights of steps in a tier of seats reserved for guests of honor" (McRay, 1991, p. 204).

The Latin inscription on the stone, however, proved that originally, it was not meant to be used as a building block in the theater. On the stone, the researchers found what was left of an inscription bearing the name of Pontius Pilate. The entire inscription is not legible, but concerning the name of Pilate, Finegan noted: "The name Pontius Pilate is quite unmistakable and is of much importance as the first epigraphical documentation concerning Pontius Pilate, who governed Judea A.D. 26-36 according to commonly accepted dates" (1992, p. 139). What the complete inscription once said is not definitely known, but there is general agreement that the stone originally may have come from a temple or shrine dedicated to the Roman emperor Tiberius (Blaiklock, 1984, p. 57). A stronger piece of evidence for the New Testament's accuracy would be difficult to find. Now appropriately known as "The Pilate Inscription," this stone slab documents that Pilate was the Roman official governing Judea, and even uses his more complete name of Pontius Pilate, as found in Luke 3:1.

CONCERNING DEATH BY CRUCIFIXION

Throughout centuries of history, crucifixion has been one of the most painful and shameful ways to die. Because of the ignominy attached to this means of death, many rulers crucified those who rebelled against them. Historically, multiplied thousands have been killed by this form of corporal punishment. John McRay, in a brief summary of several of the most notable examples of mass crucifixion, commented that Alexander Jannaeus crucified 800 Jews in Jerusalem, the Romans crucified 6,000 slaves during the revolt led by Spartacus, and Josephus saw "many" Jews crucified in Tekoe at the end of the first revolt (1991, p. 389). Yet, in spite of all the literary documentation concerning crucifixion, little, if any, physical archaeological evidence had been produced from the Bible lands concerning the practice. As with many of the people, places, and events recorded in the Bible, the lack of this physical evidence was not due to a fabrication by the biblical author, but was due, instead, to a lack of archaeological discovery.

In 1968, Vassilios Tzaferis found the first indisputable remains of a crucifixion victim. The victim's skeleton had been placed in an ossuary that "was typical of those used by Jews in the Holy Land between the end of the second century B.C. and the fall of Jerusalem in A.D. 70" (McRay, 1991, p. 204). From an analysis of the skeletal remains of the victim, osteologists and other medical professionals from the Hadassah Medical School in Jerusalem determined that the victim was a male between the approximate ages of 24 and 28 who was about five feet six inches tall. Based on the inscription of the ossuary, his name seems to have been "Yehohanan, the son of Hagakol," although the last word of the description is still disputed (p. 204). The most significant piece of the victim's skeleton is his right heel bone, because a large spike-like nail had been hammered through it. Between the head of the nail and the heel bone several fragments of olive wood were found lodged. Randall Price, in his book, *The Stones Cry Out*, suggested that the nail apparently hit a knot in the olive stake upon which this man was crucified, causing the nail and heel to be removed together, due to the difficulty of removing the nail by itself (1997, p. 309). [A full-color photograph of the feet portion of the skeleton (showing the nail) can be found in an article titled "Search for the Sacred" by Jerry Adler and Anne Underwood in the August 30, 2004 issue of *Newsweek* magazine (144[9]:38).]

As to the significance of this find, Price has provided an excellent summary. In years gone by, certain scholars believed that the story of Jesus' crucifixion had several flaws, to say the least. First, it was believed that nails were not used to secure victims to the actual cross, but that ropes were used instead for this purpose. Finding the heel bone with a several-inch-long spike intact, along with the fragments of olive wood, is indicative of the fact that the feet of crucifixion victims were attached to the cross using nails. Second, it had been suggested that victims of crucifixion were not given a decent burial. Certain scholars even suggested that the story of Jesus' burial in the tomb of Joseph of Arimathea was contrived, since crucifixion victims like Jesus were thrown into common graves alongside other condemned prisoners. The burial of the crucified victim found by Tzaferis proves that, at least on certain occasions, crucifixion victims were given a proper Jewish burial (1997, pp. 308-311; cf. Adler and Underwood, 2004, 144[9]:39).

POLITARCHS IN THESSALONICA

When writing about the Christians in Thessalonica who were accused of turning "the world upside down," Luke noted that some of the brethren were brought before the "rulers of the city" (Acts 17:5-6). The phrase "rulers of the city" (NKJV, ASV; "city authorities"–NASV) is translated from the Greek word *politarchas*, and occurs only in Acts 17 verses 6 and 8. For many years, critics of the Bible's claim of divine inspiration accused Luke of a historical inaccuracy because he used the title *politarchas* to refer to the city officials of Thessalonica, rather than employing the more common terms, *strateegoi* (magistrates) or *exousiais* (authorities). To support their accusations, they simply pointed out that the term *politarch* is found nowhere else in Greek literature as an official title. Thus, they reasoned that Luke made a mistake. How could someone refer to such an office if it did not exist? Whoever heard or read of *politarchas* in the Greek language? No one in modern times. That is, no one in modern times had heard of it until it was found recorded in the various cities of Macedonia–the province in which Thessalonica was located.

In 1960, Carl Schuler published a list of 32 inscriptions bearing the term *politarchas.* Approximately 19 of those inscriptions came from Thessalonica, and at least three of them dated back to the first century (McRay, 1991, p. 295). On the Via Egnatia, a main thoroughfare running through ancient Thessalonica, there once stood a Roman Arch called the Vardar Gate. In 1867, the arch was torn down and used to repair the city walls (p. 295). An inscription on this arch, now housed in the British Museum, ranks as one of the most important when dealing with the term *politarchas.* This particular inscription, probably dated somewhere between 30 B.C. and A.D. 143 begins with the phrase "In the time of Politarchas..." (Finegan, 1959, p. 352). Thus, most likely the arch was standing when Luke wrote his historical narrative known as Acts of the Apostles. And the fact that politarchs ruled Thessalonica during the travels of Paul now stands as indisputable.

SERGIUS PAULUS, THE PROCONSUL OF CYPRUS

Throughout Paul's missionary journeys, he and his fellow travelers came in contact with many prestigious people—including Roman rulers of the area in which the missionaries were preaching. If Luke had been fabricating these travels, he could have made vague references to Roman rulers without giving specific names and titles. But that is not what one finds in the book of Acts. On the contrary, it seems that Luke went out of his way to pinpoint specific names, titles, places, and cities. Because of this copious documentation, we have ample instances in which to check his reliability as a historian.

One such instance is found in Acts 13. In that chapter, Luke documented Paul's journey into Seleucia, then Cyprus, and Salamis, then Paphos. In Paphos, Paul and his companions encountered two individuals, a Jew named Bar-Jesus, and his "proconsul" companion Sergius Paulus, an intelligent man who summoned Paul and Barnabas in order to hear the Word of God (Acts 13:4-7). This particular reference to Sergius Paulus provides the student of archaeology with a two-fold test of Luke's accuracy. First, was the area of Cyprus and Paphos ruled by a proconsul during the time of Paul's work there? Second, was there ever a Sergius Paulus?

For many years, skeptics of Luke's accuracy claimed that the area of Cyprus would not have been ruled by a proconsul. Since Cyprus was an imperial province, it would have been put under a "propraetor" not a proconsul (Unger, 1962, pp. 185-186). While it is true that Cyprus at one time had been an imperial province, it is not true that it was such during Paul's travels there. In fact, "in 22 B.C. Augustus transferred it to the Roman Senate, and it was therefore placed under the administration of proconsuls" (Free and Vos, 1992, p. 269). Biblical scholar F.F. Bruce expanded on this information when he explained that Cyprus was made an imperial province in 27 B.C., but that Augustus gave it to the Senate five years later in exchange for Dalmatia. Once given to the Senate, proconsuls would have ruled Cyprus, just as in the other senatorial provinces (Bruce, 1990, p. 295). As Thomas Eaves remarked:

> As we turn to the writers of history for that period, Dia Cassius (*Roman History*) and Strabo (*The*

Geography of Strabo), we learn that there were two periods of Cyprus' history: first, it was an imperial province governed by a propraetor, and later in 22 B.C., it was made a senatorial province governed by a proconsul. Therefore, the historians support Luke in his statement that Cyprus was ruled by a proconsul, for it was between 40-50 A.D. when Paul made his first missionary journey. If we accept secular history as being true we must also accept Biblical history, for they are in agreement (1980, p. 234).

In addition to the known fact that Cyprus became a senatorial province, archaeologists have found copper coins from the region that refer to other proconsuls who were not much removed from the time of Paul. One such coin, called appropriately a "copper proconsular coin of Cyprus," pictures the head of Claudius Caesar, and contains the title of "Arminius Proclus, Proconsul... of the Cyprians" ("Cyprus," 1968, p. 627).

Even more impressive than the fact that Luke had the specific title recorded accurately, is the fact that evidence has come to light that the record of Sergius Paulus is equally accurate. It is interesting, in this regard, that there are several inscriptions that could possibly match the proconsul recorded by Luke. The *International Standard Bible Encyclopedia* (ISBE) records three ancient inscriptions that could be possible matches (see Hughes, 1986, 2:728). First, at Soli on the north coast of Cyprus, an inscription was uncovered that mentioned Paulus, who was a proconsul. The authors and editors of the ISBE contend that the earliest this inscription can be dated is A.D. 50, and that it therefore cannot fit the Paulus of Acts 13. Others, however, are convinced that this is the Paulus of Acts' fame (Unger, 1962, pp. 185-186, see also McGarvey, n.d., 2:7).

In addition to this find, another Latin inscription has been discovered that refers to a Lucius Sergius Paulus who was "one of the curators of the Banks of the Tiber during the reign of Claudius." Eminent archaeologist Sir William Ramsay argued that this man later became the proconsul of Cyprus, and should be connected with Acts 13 (Hughes, 2:728). Finally, a fragmentary Greek inscription hailing from Kythraia in northern Cyprus has been discovered that refers to a Quintus Sergius Paulus as a proconsul during the reign of Claudius (Hughes, 2:728). Regardless of which of these inscriptions actually connects to Acts 13, the evidence provides a plausible match. At least two men named Paulus were proconsuls in Cyprus, and at least two men named Sergius Paulus were officials during the reign of Claudius. Luke's accuracy is once again confirmed.

COUNTING QUIRINIUS

The precision with which Luke reported historical detail has been documented over and over again throughout the centuries by archaeologists and biblical scholars. In every instance, where sufficient archaeological evidence has surfaced, Luke has been vindicated as an accurate and meticulously precise writer. Skeptics and critics have been unable to verify even one anachronism or discrepancy with which to discredit the biblical writers' claims of being governed by an overriding divine influence.

However, observe the above-stated criterion that serves as the key to a fair and proper assessment of Luke's accuracy: **where sufficient archaeological evidence has surfaced**. Skeptics frequently level charges against Luke and the other biblical writers on the basis of **arguments from silence**. They fail to distinguish between a genuine contradiction on the one hand, and insufficient evidence from which to draw a firm conclusion on the other. A charge of contradiction or inaccuracy within the Bible is illegitimate and, therefore, unsustained in those areas where evidence of historical corroboration is either absent or scant.

In light of these principles, consider the following words of Luke: "And it came to pass in those days that a decree went out from Caesar Augustus that all the world should be registered. This census first took place while Quirinius was governing Syria" (Luke 2:1-2). Some scholars have charged Luke with committing an error on the basis of the fact that history records that Publius Sulpicius Quirinius was Governor of Syria beginning in A.D. 6–several years **after** the birth of Christ. It is true that thus far no historical record has surfaced to verify either the governorship or the census of Quirinius as represented by Luke at the time of Jesus' birth prior to the death of Herod in 4 B.C. As distinguished biblical archaeologist G. Ernest Wright of Harvard Divinity School conceded: "This chronological problem has not been solved" (1960, p. 158).

This void in extant information that would provide definitive archaeological confirmation notwithstanding, sufficient evidence **does** exist to postulate a plausible explanation for Luke's allusions, thereby rendering the charge of discrepancy ineffectual. Being the meticulous historian that he was, Luke demonstrated his awareness of a separate provincial census during Quirinius' governorship beginning in A.D. 6 (Acts 5:37). In view of this familiarity, he surely would not have confused this census with one taken ten or more years earlier. Hence Luke claimed that a **prior** census was, indeed, taken at the command of Caesar Augustus sometime prior to 4 B.C. He flagged this earlier census by using the expression *prote egeneto* ("first took place")—which assumes a later one (cf. Nicoll, n.d., 1:471). To question the authenticity of this claim, simply because no explicit reference has yet been found, is unwarranted and prejudicial. No one questions the historicity of the second census taken by Quirinius around A.D. 6/7, despite the fact that the sole authority for it is a single inscription found in Venice. Sir William Ramsay, world-renowned and widely acclaimed authority on such matters, wrote over one hundred years ago: "[W]hen we consider how purely accidental is the evidence for the second census, the want of evidence for the first seems to constitute no argument against the trustworthiness of Luke's statement" (1897, p. 386).

In addition, historical sources indicate that Quirinius was favored by Augustus, and was in active service of the emperor in the vicinity of Syria previous to, and during, the time period that Jesus was born. It is reasonable to conclude that Quirinius could have been appointed by Caesar to instigate a census/enrollment during that time frame, and that his competent execution of such could have earned for him a repeat appointment for the A.D. 6/7 census (see Archer, 1982, p. 366).

Notice also that Luke did not use the term *legatus*–the normal title for a Roman governor. He used the participial form of *hegemon* that was used for a propraetor (senatorial governor), or procurator (like Pontius Pilate), or quaestor (imperial commissioner) [McGarvey and Pendleton, n.d., p. 28]. After providing a thorough summary of the historical and archaeological data pertaining to this question, Finegan concluded: "Thus the situation presupposed in Luke 2:3 seems entirely plausible" (1959, 2:261). Indeed it does.

GALLIO THE PROCONSUL OF ACHAIA

Acts chapter 18 opens with a description of Paul's ministry in the city of Corinth. It was there that he contacted Aquila and his faithful wife Priscilla who had been expelled from Rome at the command of Claudius, and who, as a result, had come to live in Corinth. Due to the fact that they were tentmakers, like Paul, the apostle stayed with them and worked as a "vocational minister," making tents and preaching the Gospel. As was usually the case with Paul's preaching, many of the Jews were offended, and opposed his work. Because of this opposition, Paul told the Jews that from then on he would go to the Gentiles. That said, Paul went to the house of a man named Justus who lived next door to the synagogue. Soon after his proclamation to go to the Gentiles, Paul had a vision in which the Lord instructed him to speak boldly, because no one in the city would attack him. Encouraged by the vision, Paul continued in Corinth for a year and six months, teaching the Word of God among the people.

After Paul's eighteen-month stay in Corinth, the opposition to his preaching finally erupted into violent, political action. Acts 18:12-17 explains.

> When Gallio was proconsul of Achaia, the Jews with one accord rose up against Paul and brought him to the judgment seat, saying, "This fellow persuades men to worship God contrary to the law." And when Paul was about to open his mouth, Gallio said to the Jews, "If it were a matter of wrongdoing or wicked crimes, O Jews, there would be reason why I should bear with you. But if it is a question of words and names and your own law, look to it yourselves; for I do not want to be a judge of such matters." And he drove them from the judgment seat. Then all the Greeks took Sosthenes, the ruler of the synagogue, and beat him before the judgment seat. But Gallio took no notice of these things.

From this brief pericope of Scripture, we learn several things about Gallio and his personality. Of paramount importance to our discussion is the fact that Luke recorded that Gallio was the "proconsul of Achaia." Here again, Luke, in recording specific information about the political rulers of his day, provided his readers with a checkable point of reference. Was Gallio ever really the proconsul of Achaia?

Marianne Bonz, the former managing editor of the *Harvard Theological Review*, shed some light on a now-famous inscription concerning Gallio. She recounted how, in 1905, a doctoral student in Paris was sifting through a collection of inscriptions that had been collected from the Greek city of Delphi. In these various inscriptions, he found four different fragments that, when put together, formed a large portion of a letter from the Emperor Claudius. The letter from the emperor was written to none other than Gallio, the proconsul of Achaia (Bonz, 1998, p. 8).

McRay, in giving the Greek portions of this now-famous inscription, and supplying missing letters in the gaps of the text to make it legible, translated it as follows: "Tiberius Claudius Caesar Augustus Germanicus, Pontifex Maximus, of tribunician authority for the twelfth time, imperator twenty-sixth time...Lucius Junius Gallio, my friend, and the proconsul of Achaia" (1991, pp. 226-227). And while certain portions of the above inscription are not entirely clear, the name of Gallio and his office in Achaia are clearly legible. Not only did Luke record the name of Gallio accurately, but he also recorded his political office with equal precision.

The importance of the Gallio inscription goes even deeper than verification of Luke's accuracy. This particular find shows how archaeology can give us a better understanding of the biblical text, especially in areas of chronology. Most scholars familiar with the travels and epistles of the apostle Paul will readily admit that attaching specific dates to his activities remains an exceedingly difficult task. The Gallio inscription, however, has added a small piece to this chronological puzzle. Jack Finegan, in his detailed work on biblical chronology, dated the inscription to the year A.D. 52, Gallio's proconsulship in early A.D. 51, and Paul's arrival in Corinth in the winter of A.D. 49/50. Finegan stated concerning his conclusion: "This determination of the time when Paul arrived in Corinth thus provides an important anchor point for the entire chronology of Paul" (1998, p. 391-393).

A WORD ABOUT OSSUARIES

The *Archaeological Encyclopedia of the Holy Land* provides an excellent brief description of ossuaries in general. The writers explain that an ossuary is a small box about 2.5 feet long, usually made out of clay or cut out of chalk or limestone, primarily used to bury human bones after the soft tissue and flesh had decomposed. They "are typical of the burial practices in Jerusalem and its vicinity during the Early Roman period, i.e., between *circa* 40 B.C. and A.D. 135. Ossuaries found in the Herodian cemetery in Jericho are dated by Hachlili to a more restricted time period of between A.D. 10-68" ("Ossuary," 2001, p. 377). Ossuary panels often had decorations on them, and many had inscriptions or painted markings and letters, indicating whose bones were inside.

Of interest is the fact that many of the ossuaries discovered to date contain the same names that we find in the biblical account. And, while we cannot be sure that the bones contained in the ossuaries are the bones of the exact personalities mentioned in the Bible, the matching nomenclature does show that the biblical writers at least used names that coincided accurately with the names used in general during the time that the New Testament books were written.

Coming down the direct descent on the Mount of Olives is the site known as *Dominus flevit*, "the name embodying the tradition that this is the place where 'the Lord wept' over Jerusalem" (Finegan, 1992, p. 171). In 1953, excavations began in this area, and a large cemetery was discovered, consisting of at least five hundred known burial places. Among these many burial sites, over 120 ossuaries were discovered, more than 40 of which contained inscriptions and writing. Among the labeled ossuaries, the names of Martha and Miriam appear on a single ossuary. Other names that appear on the ossuaries are Joseph, Judas, Solome, Sapphira, Simeon, Yeshua (Jesus), Zechariah, Eleazar, Jairus, and John (Finegan, 1992, pp. 366-371). Free and Vos, in their brief critique of Rudolph Bultmann's "form criticism," used ossuary evidence to expose a few of the flaws in Bultmann's ideas. They wrote: "[S]ome scholars formerly held that personal names used in the gospels, particularly in John, were fictitious and had been selected because of their meaning and not because they referred to historical persons. Such speculations are not supported by the ossuary inscriptions, which preserve many of the biblical names" (1992, p. 256).

Along these same lines, Price discussed several ossuaries that were found accidentally in 1990, when workers were building a water park in Jerusalem's Peace Forest. Among the twelve limestone ossuaries discovered, one "was exquisitely ornate and decorated with incised rosette. Obviously it had belonged to a wealthy or high-ranking patron who could afford such a box. On this box was an inscription. It read in two places *Qafa* and *Yehosef bar Qayafa* ('Caiphas,' 'Joseph, son of Caiphas')" (1997, p. 305). Price connected this Caiphas to the one recorded in the Bible, using two lines of reasoning. First, the Caiphas in the biblical record was an influential, prominent high priest who would have possessed the means to obtain such an ornate burial box. Second, while the New Testament text gives only the name Caiphas, Josephus "gives his full name as 'Joseph who was called Caiaphas of the high priesthood'" (p. 305). Of further interest is the fact that the ossuary contained the bones of six different people, one of which was a man around the age of 60. Are these the bones of the Caiaphas recorded in the New Testament? No one can be sure. It is the case, however, that many ossuary finds, at the very least, verify that the New Testament writers used names that were common during the period in which they wrote.

A note of caution is needed regarding attempts to prove a direct connection between ossuary finds and biblical characters. One of the most famous of such attempts thus far comes from the "James" ossuary that captured the world's attention in late 2002. The inscription on that particular bone box reads: "James, the son of Joseph, brother of Jesus." Was this the ossuary that contained the bones of Jesus Christ's physical brother? In 2002, the answer remained to be seen. In a brief article I authored on this matter in December 2002, I wrote: "At present, we cannot be dogmatic about the ossuarial evidence" (Butt, 2002). Currently, the inscription still finds itself embroiled in debate. After analyzing the inscription, a committee appointed by the Israeli Antiquities Authority declared it to be unauthentic. According to Eric Myers, a Judai-studies scholar at Duke University, "the overwhelming scholarly consensus is that it's a fake" (as quoted in Adler and Underwood, 2004, 144[9]:38). However, Hershel Shanks, the distinguished editor of *Biblical Archaeology Review*, insists that the inscription remains antiquated and may possibly be linked to the Jesus and James of the Bible (Shanks, 2004; cf. Adler and Underwood, p. 38).

Whether or not the inscription is authentic remains to be seen. Yet, even if the inscription does prove to date to around the first century, that still would not prove that the ossuary contained the bones of Jesus' physical brother. It would prove that names like Joseph, James, and Jesus were used during that time in that region of the world. This would, at the very least, verify that the biblical writers related information that fit with the events happening at the time they produced their writings. As Andrew Overman, head of classics at Macalester College, stated: "Even if the [James] Ossuary is genuine, it provides no new information" (Adler and Underwood, p. 39).

Another famous ossuary connection to the biblical text was the tomb that documentary filmmakers James Cameron and Simcha Jacobovici alleged to be the lost tomb of Jesus–complete with His bones in an ancient ossuary. This outlandish claim has been thoroughly refuted (see Bryant, 2007). Furthermore, Cameron and Jacobovici's use of scanty archaeological information highlights the fact that caution must be used when attempting to make direct archaeological connections to the Bible.

When looking to archaeology, we must avoid asking it to prove too much. The discipline does have limitations. Yet, in spite of those limitations, it remains a valuable tool that can be used to shed light on the biblical text. As Adler and Underwood remarked, the value of archaeology is "in providing a historical and intellectual context, and the occasional flash of illumination on crucial details" (p. 39).

GENTILES AND THE TEMPLE

Near the end of the book of Acts, the apostle Paul was making every effort to arrive in the city of Jerusalem in time to celebrate an upcoming Jewish feast. Upon reaching Jerusalem, he met with James and several of the Jewish leaders, and reported "those things which God had done among the Gentiles through his ministry" (Acts 21:19). Upon hearing Paul's report, the Jewish leaders of the church advised Paul to take certain men into the temple and purify himself along with the men. While in the temple, certain Jews from Asia saw Paul, and stirred up the crowd against him, saying, "Men of Israel, help! This is the man who teaches all men everywhere against the people, the law, and this place; and furthermore he also brought Greeks into the temple and has defiled this holy place" (Acts 21:28). In the next verse, the inspired text relates the fact that the men had seen Trophimus the Ephesian with Paul in the city, and they "supposed" Paul had brought him into the temple (although the record does not indicate that anyone actually **saw** this happen).

In response to the accusation that Paul had defiled the temple by bringing in a Gentile, the text states that "all the city was disturbed; and the people ran together, seized Paul, and dragged him out of the temple; and immediately the doors were shut" (Acts 21:30). The next verse of Acts states explicitly what this violent mob planned to do with Paul: "Now as they were seeking to kill him, news came to the commander of the garrison that all Jerusalem was in an uproar." Under what law or pretense was the Jewish mob working when they intended to kill Paul?

A plausible answer to this question comes to us from archaeology. In his description of the temple in Jerusalem, Josephus explained that a certain inscription separated the part of the temple that the Gentiles **could** enter, from the parts of the temple that Gentiles **could not** enter. This inscription, says Josephus, "forbade any foreigner to go in, under pain of death" (*Antiquities*, 15:11:5). A find published in 1871 by C.S. Clermont-Ganneau brings the picture into clearer focus. About 50 meters from the actual temple site, a fragment of stone with seven lines of Greek capitals was discovered (Thompson, 1962, p. 314). Finegan gives the entire Greek text, and translates the inscription as follows: "No foreigner is to enter within the balustrade and enclosure around the temple area. Whoever is caught will have himself to blame for his death which will follow" (1992, p. 197).

In addition to this single inscription, another stone fragment was found and described in 1938. Discovered near the north gate of Jerusalem, also known as St. Stephen's Gate, this additional stone fragment was smaller than the first, and had only six lines instead of seven. The partially preserved words clearly coincided with those on the previous inscription. Finegan noted concerning the preserved words: "From them it would appear that the wording of the entire inscription was identical (except for *aut*) instead of *eautoo...*" (1992, p. 197). [NOTE: Finegan mentioned that the letters of this second inscription had been painted red, and the letters still retained much of their original coloration.]

In light of these finds, and the comments by Josephus, one can see why the mob in Acts 21 so boldly sought to kill Paul. These inscriptions shed light on the biblical text, and in doing so, offer further confirmation of its accuracy.

CORBAN

On several occasions, Jesus was accosted by the Pharisees and other religious leaders, because He and His disciples were not doing exactly what the Pharisees thought they should be doing. Many times, the religious leaders had instituted laws or traditions that were not in God's Word, but nonetheless were treated with equal or greater reverence than the laws given by God. In Mark 7:1-16, the Bible records that the Pharisees and other leaders were finding fault with the disciples of Jesus because Jesus' followers did not wash their hands in the traditional manner before they ate. The Pharisees said to Jesus: "Why do your disciples not walk according to the tradition of the elders, but eat bread with unwashed hands?" (Mark 7:5).

Upon hearing this accusatory interrogation, Jesus launched into a powerful condemnation of the accusers. Jesus explained that His inquisitors often kept **their** beloved traditions, while ignoring the commandments of God. Jesus said: "All too well you reject the commandment of God, that you may keep your tradition" (Mark 7:9). As a case in point of their rejection of God's Law, Jesus went on to say:

> For Moses said, "Honor your father and your mother"; and, "He who curses father or mother,

let him be put to death." But you say, "If a man says to his father or mother, 'Whatever profit you might have received from me is **Corban'** (that is, a gift to God)," then you no longer let him do anything for his father or his mother, making the word of God of no effect through your tradition which you have handed down. And many such things you do (Mark 7:11-13, emp. added).

In this passage, Jesus repudiated the Pharisees' ungodly insistence upon their own traditions, and at the same time included a reference that can be (and has been) authenticated by archaeological discovery. Jesus mentioned the word *corban*, a word that the writer of the gospel account felt needed a little explanation. Mark defined the word as "a gift to God." In a discussion of this term in an article by Kathleen and Leen Ritmeyer, the word comes into sharper focus. They documented a fragment of a stone vessel found near the southern wall of the temple. On the fragment, the Hebrew word *krbn* (korban–the same word used by Jesus in Mark 7) is inscribed (1992, p. 41).

Of further interest is the fact that the inscription also included "two crudely drawn birds, identified as pigeons or doves." The authors mentioned that the vessel might have been "used in connection with a sacrifice to celebrate the birth of a child" (Ritmeyer, 1992, p. 41). In Luke 2:24, we read about Joseph and Mary offering two pigeons when they took baby Jesus to present Him to God. Since these animals were the prescribed sacrifice for certain temple sacrifices, those who sold them set up shop in the temple. Due to the immoral practices of many such merchants, they fell under Jesus' attack when He cleansed the temple and "overturned the tables of the moneychangers and seats of those who sold doves" (Mark 11:15).

CONCLUSION

Over and over, biblical references that can be checked prove to be historically accurate in every detail. After hundreds of years of critical scrutiny, both the Old and New Testaments of the Bible have proven their authenticity and accuracy at every turn. Sir William Ramsay, in his assessment of Luke's writings in the New Testament, wrote: "You may press the words of Luke in a degree beyond any other historian's, and they stand the keenest scrutiny and the hardest treatment, provided always that the critic knows the subject and does not go beyond the limits of science and of justice" (1915, p. 89). Now, almost a hundred years after that statement originally was written, the exact same thing can be said with even more certainty of the writings of Luke–and every other Bible writer. Almost 3,000 years ago, the sweet singer of Israel, in his description of God's Word, put it perfectly when he said: "The entirety of Your word is truth" (Psalm 119:160).

CHAPTER 7

SCIENTIFIC FOREKNOWLEDGE AND MEDICAL ACUMEN OF THE BIBLE

While it is the case that the Bible does not present itself as a scientific or medical textbook, it is only reasonable that if God truly did inspire the books that compose the Bible, they would be completely accurate in every scientific or medical detail found among their pages. Furthermore, if the omniscient Ruler of the Universe actually did inspire these books, scientific and medical errors that fill the pages of other ancient, non-inspired texts should be entirely absent from the biblical record. Is the Bible infallible when it speaks about scientific fields of discipline, or does it contain the errors that one would expect to find in the writings of fallible men in ancient times?

That the first five books of the Old Testament are a product of Moses is a matter of historical record (Lyons and Smith, 2003). Furthermore, the story of Moses' education among the Egyptian culture was well understood. In fact, even those Jews who did not convert to Christianity were so familiar with the historic fact that Moses was educated in "all the wisdom of the Egyptians" (Acts 7:22), that Stephen's statement to that effect went completely undisputed. Moses had been trained under the most advanced Egyptian educational system of his day. With such training, it would have been only natural for Moses to include some of the Egyptian "wisdom" in his writings if he were composing the Pentateuch by using his own prowess and mental faculties.

A look into the medical practices from ancient Egypt and those found in the Pentateuch, however, reveals that Moses did not necessarily rely on "wisdom" of the Egyptians (which, in many cases, consisted of life-threatening malpractice). While some medical practices in the Pentateuch are similar to those found in ancient Egyptian documents, the Pentateuch exhibits a conspicuous absence of those harmful malpractices that plague the writings of the Egyptians. Moses penned the most advanced, flawless medical prescriptions that had ever been recorded. Furthermore, every statement that pertained to the health and medical well-being of the Israelite nation recorded by Moses could theoretically still be implemented and be completely in accord with every fact modern medicine has learned in regard to germ spreading, epidemic disease control, communal sanitation, and a host of other medical and scientific discoveries.

It is the case that the ancient Egyptians were renowned in the ancient world for their progress in the field of medicine. Dr. Massengill noted that "Egypt was the medical center of the ancient world" (1943, p. 13). During the days of in the Medo-Persian Empire, the ancient historian Herodotus recorded that it was king Darius' practice "to keep in attendance certain Egyptian doctors, who had a reputation for the highest eminence in their profession" (3.129). Thus, while the medical practices of the Bible could be equally compared to those of other ancient cultures and found to be flawlessly superior, comparing them to that of the eminent Egyptian culture should suffice to manifest the Bible's supernatural superiority in the field.

It Will Cure You—If It Doesn't Kill You First

Among the ancient documents that detail much of the Egyptian medicinal knowledge, the Ebers Papyrus ranks as one of the foremost sources. This papyrus was discovered in 1872 by a German Egyptologist named Georg Ebers (the name from which the papyrus acquired its moniker) (*Ancient Egyptian...*, 1930, p. 1). It consists of a host of medical remedies purported to heal, enhance, and prevent. "Altogether 811 prescriptions are set forth in the Papyrus, and they take the form of salves, plasters, and poultices; snuffs, inhalations, and gargles; draughts, confections, and pills; fumigations, suppositories, and enemata" (p. 15). Among the hundreds of prescriptions, disgusting treatments that caused much more harm than good can be found. For instance, under a section titled "What to do to draw out splinters in the flesh," a remedy is prescribed consisting of worm blood, mole, and donkey dung" (p. 73). [Doctors S.I. McMillen and David Stern note that dung "is loaded with tetanus spores" and "a simple splinter often resulted in a gruesome death from lockjaw (2000, p. 10).] Remedies to help heal skin diseases included such prescriptions as: "A hog's tooth, cat's dung, dog's dung, aau-of-samu-oil, berries-of-the-xet-plant, pound and apply as poultice" (*Ancient Egyptian...*, 1930, p. 92). Various other ingredients for the plethora of remedies concocted included "dried excrement of a child" (p.

98), "hog dung" (p. 115), and "a farmer's urine" (p. 131). One recipe to prevent hair growth included lizard dung and the blood from a cow, donkey, pig, dog, and stag (p. 102). While it must be noted that some of the Egyptian medicine actually did include prescriptions and remedies that could be helpful, the harmful remedies and ingredients cast a sickening shadow of untrustworthiness over the entire Egyptian endeavor as viewed by the modern reader.

As medical doctor S.E. Massengill stated:

> The early Egyptian physicians made considerable use of drugs. Their drugs were of the kind usually found in early civilizations; a few effective remedies lost in a mass of substances of purely superstitious origin. They used opium, squill, and other vegetable substances, but also excrement and urine. It is said that the urine of a faithful wife was with them effective in the treatment of sore eyes (1943, p. 15).

In addition, it seems that the Egyptians were among the first to present the idea of "good and laudable pus" (McMillen and Stern, 2000, p. 10). Due to the idea that infection was good and the pus that resulted from it was a welcomed effect, "well-meaning doctors killed millions by deliberately infecting their wounds" (p. 10). Needless to say, the modern-day reader would not want to be a patient in an ancient Egyptian clinic!

PRESCRIPTIONS IN THE PENTATEUCH

The first five books of the Old Testament, admittedly, are not devoted entirely to the enumeration of medical prescriptions. They are not ancient medical textbooks. These books do, however, contain numerous regulations for sanitation, quarantine, and other medical procedures that were to govern the daily lives of the Israelite nation. Missing entirely from the pages of these writings are the harmful remedies and ingredients prescribed by other ancient civilizations. In fact, the Pentateuch exhibits an understanding of germs and disease that much "modern" medicine did not grasp for 3,500 years after the books were written.

Blood: The Liquid of Life

Blood always has been a curious substance whose vast mysteries and capabilities have yet to be fully explored. Doctors in the twenty-first century transfuse it, draw it, separate it, package it, store it, ship it, and sell it. And, although modern-day scientists have not uncovered completely all of the wonders of blood, they have discovered that it is the key to life. Without this "liquid of life," humans and animals would have no way to circulate the necessary oxygen and proteins that their bodies need in order to survive and reproduce. Hemoglobin found in the red blood cells carries oxygen to the brain, which in turn uses that oxygen to control the entire body. A brain without oxygen is like a car without gas or a computer without electricity. Blood makes all of the functions in the body possible.

In the past, ignorance of blood's value caused some "learned" men to do tragic things. For instance, during the middle ages, and even until the nineteenth century, doctors believed that harmful "vapors" entered the blood and caused sickness. For this reason, leeches were applied to victims of fever and other illnesses in an attempt to draw out blood containing these vapors. Also, the veins and arteries located just above the elbow were opened, and the patient's arms were bled to expunge the contaminated blood. George Washington, the first President of the United States, died because of such misplaced medical zeal. An eyewitness account of Washington's death relates that he came down with a chill, and in an effort to cure him, those who attended him resorted to bleeding; "a vein was opened, but no relief afforded" ("The Death of George Washington," 2001).

Thousands of years before the lethal practice of bloodletting was conceived, mankind had been informed by God that blood was indeed the key to life. In Leviticus 17:11, Moses wrote: "For the life of the flesh is in the blood."

Today, we understand completely the truthfulness of Moses' statement that "the life of the flesh is in the blood." But how did an ancient shepherd like Moses come to know such information? Just a lucky guess? How could Moses have known almost 3,500 years ago that life was in the blood, while it took the rest of the scientific and medical community thousands of years (and thousands of lives!) to grasp this truth? The Old Testament's conspicuous failure to institute improper medical procedures as they related to blood speaks loudly of its medical accuracy.

Germs, Labor Fever, and Biblical Sanitation

In their book, *None of These Diseases*, physicians S.I. McMillen and David Stern discussed how many of the hygienic rules established by God for the children of Israel still are applicable today. To illustrate their point, they recounted the story of Ignaz Semmelweis.

In 1847, an obstetrician named Ignaz Semmelweis was the director of a hospital ward in Vienna, Austria. Many pregnant women checked into his ward, but 18% of them never checked out. One out of every six that received treatment in Semmelweis' ward died of labor fever (Nuland, 2003, p. 31). Autopsies revealed pus under their skin, in their chest cavities, in their eye sockets, etc. Semmelweis was distraught over the mortality rate in his ward, and other hospital wards like it all over Europe. Nuland noted that Australia, the Americas, Britain, Ireland, and practically every other nation that had established a hospital suffered a similar mortality rate (2003, pp. 41-43). If a woman delivered a baby using a midwife, then the death fell to only about 3%. Yet if she chose to use the most advanced medical knowledge and facilities of the day, her chance of dying skyrocketed immensely!

Semmelweis tried everything to curb the carnage. He turned all the women on their sides in hopes that the death rate would drop, but with no results. He thought maybe the bell that the priest rang late in the evenings scared the women, so he made the priest enter silently, yet without any drop in death rates.

As he contemplated his dilemma, he watched young medical students perform their routine tasks. Each day the students would perform autopsies on the dead mothers. Then they would rinse their hands in a bowl of bloody water, wipe them off on a common, shared towel, and immediately begin internal examinations of the still-living women. Nuland commented concerning the practice: "Because there seemed no reason for them to wash their hands, except superficially, or change their clothing before coming to the First Division, they did neither" (2003, p. 100). As a twenty-first-century observer, one is appalled to think that such practices actually took place in institutes of what was at the time "modern technology." What doctor in his right mind would touch a dead person and then perform examinations on living patients—without first employing some sort of minimal hygienic practices intended to kill germs? But to Europeans in the middle-nineteenth-century, germs were virtually a foreign concept. They never had seen a germ, much less been able to predict its destructive potential. According to many of their most prevalent theories, disease was caused by "atmospheric conditions" or "cosmic telluric influences."

Semmelweis ordered everyone in his ward to wash his or her hands thoroughly in a chlorine solution after every examination. In three months, the death rate fell from 18% to 1%. Semmelweis had made an amazing discovery. On the inside cover-flap of the book about Semmelweis, written by medical doctor and historian Sherwin Nuland, the text reads:

> Ignác Semmelweis is remembered for the now-commonplace notion that doctors must wash their hands before examining patients. In mid-nineteenth-century Vienna, this was a subversive idea. With deaths from childbed fever exploding, Semmelweis discovered that doctors themselves were spreading the disease (2003, inside cover flap).

Had Semmelweis made a groundbreaking discovery, or is it possible that he simply "rediscovered" what had been known in some circles for many years? Almost 3,300 years before Semmelweis lived, Moses had written: "He who touches the dead body of anyone shall be unclean seven days. He shall purify himself with the water on the third day and on the seventh day; then he will be clean. But if he does not purify himself on the third day and on the seventh day, he will not be clean." Germs were no new discovery in 1847; the biblical text recorded measures to check their spread as far back as approximately 1500 B.C.

The Water of Purification

Also germane to this discussion is the composition of the "water of purification" listed in Numbers 19. When Old Testament instructions are compared to the New Testament explanations for those actions, it becomes clear that some of the ancient injunctions were primarily symbolic in nature. For instance, when the Passover Lamb was eaten, none of its bones was to be broken. This symbolized the sacrifice of Christ, Whose side was pierced, yet even in death escaped the usual practice of having His legs broken (John 19:31-37).

With the presence of such symbolism in the Old Testament, it is important that we do not overlook the Old Testament instructions that were pragmatic in value and that testify to a Master Mind behind the writing of the Law. One such directive is found in Numbers 19, where the Israelites were instructed to prepare the "water of purification" that was to be used to wash any person who had touched a dead body.

At first glance, the water of purification sounds like a hodge-podge of superstitious potion-making that included the ashes of a red heifer, hyssop, cedar wood, and scarlet. But this formula was the farthest thing from a symbolic potion intended to "ward off evil spirits." On the contrary, the recipe for the water of purification stands today as a wonderful example of the Bible's brilliance, since the recipe is nothing less than a procedure to produce an antibacterial soap.

When we look at the ingredients individually, we begin to see the value of each. First, consider the ashes of a red heifer and cedar. As most school children know, the pioneers in this country could not go to the nearest supermarket and buy their favorite personal hygiene products. If they needed soap or shampoo, they made it themselves. Under such situations, they concocted various recipes for soap. One of the most oft'-produced types of soap was lye soap. Practically anyone today can easily obtain a recipe for lye soap via a quick search of the Internet (see "Soapmaking," n.d.). The various lye-soap recipes reveal that, to obtain lye, water often is poured through ashes. The water retrieved from pouring it through the ashes contains a concentration of lye. Lye, in high concentrations, is very caustic and irritating to the skin. It is, in fact, one of the main ingredients in many modern chemical mixtures used to unclog drains. In more diluted concentrations, it can be used as an excellent exfoliant and cleansing agent. Many companies today still produce lye soaps. Amazingly, Moses instructed the Israelites to prepare a mixture that would have included lye mixed in a diluted solution.

Furthermore, consider that hyssop was also added to the "water of purification." Hyssop contains the antiseptic thymol, the same ingredient that we find today in some brands of mouthwash (McMillen and Stern, 2000, p. 24). Hyssop oil continues to be a popular "healing oil," and actually is quite expensive. In listing the benefits of hyssop, one Web site noted: "Once used for purifying temples and cleansing lepers, the leaves contain an antiseptic, antiviral oil. A mold that produces penicillin grows on the leaves. An infusion is taken as a sedative expectorant for flue, bronchitis, and phlegm" (see "Hyssop").

Other ingredients in the "water of purification" also stand out as having beneficial properties. The oil from the cedar wood in the mixture most likely maintained numerous salutary properties. A Web site dealing with various essential oils noted: "Cedar wood has long been used for storage cabinets because of its ability to repel insects and prevent decay. In oil form, applied to humans, it is an antiseptic, astringent, expectorant (removes mucus from respiratory system), anti-fungal, sedative and insecticide" ("Spa Essential Oils," 2005). Another site, more specifically dealing with the beneficial properties of cedar, explained:

> Cedar leaves and twigs are in fact rich in vitamin C, and it was their effectiveness in preventing or treating scurvy that led to the tree's being called arbor vitae or tree of life. In addition, recent research has shown that extracts prepared from either *Thuja occidentalis* or *Thuja plicata* [types of oriental cedar–KB] do in fact have antiviral, anti-inflammatory, and antibacterial properties. A group of German researchers reported in 2002 that an extract prepared from cedar leaf, alcohol, and water inhibits the reproduction of influenza virus type A, while a team of researchers in Japan found that an extract of Western red cedar was effective in treating eczema (Frey, n.d).

It is interesting to note that this information about the beneficial properties of the ingredients such as cedar, hyssop, and lye in the water of purification is not coming from Bible-based sources. Most of it is simply coming from studies that have been done through cosmetic and therapeutic research.

Finally, the Israelites were instructed to toss into the mix "scarlet," which most likely was scarlet wool (see Hebrews 9:19). Adding wool fibers to the concoction would have made the mixture the "ancient equivalent of Lava® soap" (McMillen and Stern, 2000, p. 25).

Thousands of years before any formal studies were done to see what type of cleaning methods were the most effective; millennia before American pioneers concocted their lye solutions; and ages before our most advanced medical students knew a thing about germ theory, Moses instructed the Israelites to concoct an amazingly effective recipe for soap, that, if used properly in medical facilities like hospitals in Vienna, would literally have saved thousands of lives.

Quarantine

Moses detailed measures to prevent the spread of germs from dead bodies to living humans long before such was understood and prescribed in modern medicine. But the Old Testament record added another extremely beneficial practice to the field of medicine in its detailed descriptions of maladies for which living individuals should be quarantined. The book of Leviticus lists a plethora of diseases and ways in which an Israelite would come in contact with germs. Those with such diseases as leprosy were instructed to "dwell alone" "outside the camp" (Leviticus 13:46). If and when a diseased individual did get close to those who were not diseased, he was instructed to "cover his mustache, and cry, 'Unclean! Unclean!'" (13:45). It is of interest that the covering of ones mustache would prevent spit and spray from the mouth of the individual to pass freely through the air, much like the covering of one's mouth during a cough.

Concerning such quarantine practices, S.E. Massengill wrote in his book *A Sketch of Medicine and Pharmacy*:

> In the prevention of disease, however, the ancient Hebrews made real progress. The teachings of Moses, as embodied in the Priestly Code of the Old Testament, contain two clear conceptions of modern sanitation—the importance of cleanliness and the possibility of controlling epidemic disease by isolation and quarantine (1943, p. 252).

In regard to the understanding of contagion implied in the quarantine rules in the Old Testament, McGrew noted in the *Encyclopedia of Medical History*: "The idea of contagion was foreign to the classic medical tradition and found no place in the voluminous Hippocratic writings. The Old Testament, however, is a rich source for contagionist sentiment, especially in regard to leprosy and venereal disease" (1985, pp.77-78). Here again, the Old Testament exhibits amazingly accurate medical knowledge that surpasses any known human ingenuity available at the time of its writing.

LAWS OF FOOD CONSUMPTION

Food regulations enumerated in the first five books of the Old Testament have been scrutinized by credentialed professionals in the fields of dietary and pathological research. The regulations have proven to coincide with modern science's understanding of various aspects of health and disease prevention.

In 1953, an extensive study, performed by David I. Macht and published in the *Bulletin of the History of Medicine* (a publication of the American Association of the History of Medicine and of The Johns Hopkins Institute of the History of Medicine), tested the toxicity of the meat of animals listed in Leviticus 11 and Deuteronomy 14. Macht's technique was to place a certain seedling (*Lupinus albus*) in fresh muscle juices of the various animals noted as clean and unclean in the biblical text. This method was used at the time to study the blood of normal human patients as compared to the blood of cancerous patients (1953, p. 444). Macht noted that his results revealed "data which are of considerable interest not only to the medical investigator but also to the students of ancient Biblical literature" (p. 445).

Some of his results were indeed of interest. For instance, he would take a control group of seedlings that grew in normal solutions and compare that group to seedlings placed in the various meat juices. He would then record the percent of seeds that grew in the meat juices as compared to those that grew under normal circumstances. For example, when placing the seedlings in meat juices from the Ox, the seeds grew 91% as often as they would if placed in a regular growing solution. Seeds in sheep juices grew 94% as often as those in the control group in regular solution. Seedlings in meat juice from a calf—82%; from a goat—90%; and from a deer 90%. Since these animals chew the cud and have a divided hoof, they were listed as clean in Leviticus 11 and Deuteronomy 14:

> Now the Lord spoke to Moses and Aaron, saying to them, "Speak to the children of Israel, saying, 'These are the animals which you may eat among all the animals that are on the earth: Among the animals, whatever divides the hoof, having cloven hooves and chewing the cud–that you may eat'" (Leviticus 11:1-3).

When several unclean animals were studied, however, they showed significantly higher levels of toxicity and much lower levels of seedling growth. Seedlings in meat juice from pigs grew only 54% as often as the control group under normal growing conditions; rabbit–49%; camel–41%; and horse–39%. These results for larger mammals suggested that the biblical division between clean and unclean could have been related to the toxicity of the juices of such animals.

Macht did similar research on birds, in which he found that extracts from biblical clean birds such as the pigeon and quail grew his seedlings 93% and 89%, while those from unclean birds such as the Red-tail hawk (36%) and owl (62%) were much more toxic. As Moses said: "And these you shall regard as an abomination among the birds; they shall not be eaten, they are an abomination: the eagle, the vulture, the buzzard, the kite, and the falcon after its kind; every raven after its kind, the ostrich, the short-eared owl, the sea gull, and the hawk after its kind" (Leviticus 11:13-19). Other studies included several different kinds of fish. The biblical regulation for eating fish was that the Israelites could eat any fish that had fins and scales (Deuteronomy 14:9). Those water-living creatures that did not possess fins and scales were not to be eaten (14:10). In regard to his study on the toxicity of fish, Macht wrote:

> Of special interest were experiments made with muscle juices and also blood solutions obtained from many species of fishes. Fifty-four species of fishes were so far studied in regard to toxicity of meat extracts. It was found that the muscle extracts of those fishes which possess scales and fins were practically non-toxic [Herring–100%; Pike–98%; Shad–100%–KB], while muscle extracts from fishes without scales and fins were highly toxic for the growth of Lupinus albus seedlings (pp. 446-448).

Macht's study, even after more than five decades, continues to remain of great interest. His rigorous research led him to conclude:

> The observations described above corroborate the impression repeatedly made on the author in investigations as a physician (M.D. Johns Hopkins, 1906), as an experimental biologist (Member of Society for Experimental Biology and Medicine), and as Doctor of Hebrew Literature (Yeshiva University, 1928) that all allusions of the Book of Books, to nature, natural phenomena, and natural history, whether in the form of factual statements or in the form of metaphors, similes, parables, allegories, or other tropes are correct either literally or figuratively.... Such being the extraordinary concordance between the data of the Scriptures and many of the modern and even most recent discoveries in both the biological and physico-chemical sciences, every serious student of the Bible will, I believe, endorse the assertion of Sir Isaac Newton, that "The Scriptures of God are the most sublime philosophy. I find more such

marks of authenticity in the Bible than in profane history anywhere" (p. 449).

Some, however, have questioned Macht's results. Prior research done by Macht in 1936 and 1949 produced discordant results from his research in 1953. But there are several compelling reasons for accepting Macht's 1953 research. First, it could be the case that Macht's 1953 research simply was more refined and the procedure better understood. As one would expect in the scientific field, research generally tends to improve with time. Second, Macht was a high-profile doctor with copious credentials. His research in 1936 and 1949 had been published and was easily accessible. Yet even though his previous research was available, the Johns Hopkins Institute considered it acceptable to publish his 1953 research, which would suggest that the 1953 research included additional methods and/or information that would override the earlier research. Third, Macht's procedure as described in the 1953 paper was fairly simple and easily reproducible. But those who question the work have failed to produce experimental data after 1953 that would negate Macht's study. If his 1953 procedures were fraught with error, a few simple experiments could be done to prove that. No such experimental data refuting Macht has been produced.

For these reasons, the findings of Dr. Macht aid in the defense of the Bible's inspiration and remarkably accurate medical procedures as far back as the time of Moses. But the validity of Old Testament food consumption laws certainly does not rely solely on Macht's 1953 research. Additional confirmation of the beneficial, protective nature of Mosaic food consumption laws is readily available.

Fins and Scales

As was previously mentioned, the Mosaic criteria for eating water-living creatures was that the creatures have scales and fins (Leviticus 11:12). This injunction was extremely beneficial, since a multitude of problems surround many sea creatures that do not have scales and fins.

The Blowfish

The blowfish has fins but does not have scales. Thus, it would not have been edible under the Old Testament laws–fortunately for the Israelites. The blowfish can contain toxin in its ovaries, liver, and other organs that is highly potent and deadly. This toxin, called tetrodotoxin, is thought to be "1250 times more deadly than cyanide" and 160,000 times more potent than cocaine. A tiny amount of it can kill 30 grown adults (Dilion, 2005). As odd as it sounds, blowfish is served as a delicacy all over the world, especially in Japan and other far eastern countries. As a delicacy, it is called fugu, and is prepared by certified, licensed chefs. The toxins can be removed successfully, making the food edible, but the procedure often goes awry. Some who have researched fugu say that it is a food connoisseur's version of Russian roulette. Due to the extreme danger involved in eating fugu, it is illegal to serve it to the Emperor of Japan! The Mosaic instructions concerning edible fish would have helped the Israelites avoid the dangerous blowfish, as well as danger posed by eating other toxic sea creatures such as certain jelly fish, sea anemones, and octopi.

Shellfish

Although shellfish are edible today, there are inherent dangers in eating ill-prepared types such as oysters. The U.S. Food and Drug Administration has produced a twelve-page tract warning people about the dangers of eating raw or partially cooked oysters ("Carlos' Tragic...," 2003). In the tract, the FDA warns that some raw oysters contain the bacteria *Vibrio vulnificus.* In regard to this dangerous bacteria, the tract states:

> Oysters are sometimes contaminated with the naturally occurring bacteria *Vibrio vulnificus.* Oysters contaminated with *Vibrio vulnificus* can't be detected by smell or sight; they look like other oysters. Eating raw oysters containing *Vibrio vulnificus* is very dangerous for those with pre-existing medical conditions such as liver disease, diabetes, hepatitis, cancer and HIV.... 50 percent of people who are infected with *Vibrio vulnificus* as a result of eating raw contaminated oysters die (2003).

Eating oysters if they are not cooked properly can be potentially fatal, says the FDA. Thus, the wisdom of the Mosaic prohibition is evident to an honest observer. In a time when proper handling and preparation procedures were difficult to achieve, the best course of action simply would have been to avoid the risk of eating potentially contaminated foods, especially since the contamination cannot be detected by smell or sight.

Reptiles and *Salmonella*

In Leviticus 11, Moses included reptiles in the list of unclean animals. Obviously, they are not cud-chewers that walk on cloven hooves, so they would not classify as clean, edible animals according to Leviticus 11:3. But to make sure that the Israelites understood, Moses specifically mentioned reptiles such as the large lizard, gecko, monitor lizard, sand reptile, sand lizard, and chameleon (Leviticus 11:29-31). Immediately following this listing of reptiles, the text states: "Whoever touches them when they are dead shall be unclean until evening" (11:31).

Interestingly, reptiles have a much higher rate of carrying *Salmonella* bacteria than do most mammals, especially those listed as clean in the Old Law. The Center for Disease Control has repeatedly warned people about the possibility of being infected with *Salmonella* passed through reptiles. In summarizing the CDC's 2003 report, Lianne McLeod noted that the CDC estimates over 70,000 cases of human *Salmonella* infection a year are related to the handling of reptiles and amphibians (2007). The CDC recommends that homes with children under five should not have reptiles as pets. Furthermore, while other animals such as cats and dogs can pass *Salmonella,* McLeod noted:

> As high as **90% of reptiles** are natural carriers of *Salmonella* bacteria, harboring strains specific to reptiles without any symptoms of disease in the reptile. While it is true that many pets can carry *Salmonella*, the problem with reptiles (and apparently amphibians) is that they carry *Salmonella* with such high frequency. **It is prudent to assume that all reptiles and amphibians can be a potential source of Salmonella** (2007, emp. added).

In light of such evidence, the prudence of the Mosaic prohibition to eat or handle reptile carcasses is clearly evident.

Of further interest is the fact that reptilian *Salmonella* contamination can occur without even touching a reptile. If a person touches something that has touched a reptile the bacteria can spread. The ARAV (Association of Reptilian and Amphibian Veterinarians) made this statement: "*Salmonella* bacteria are easily spread from reptiles to humans. Humans may become infected when they place their hands on objects, including food items, that have been in contact with the stool of reptiles, in their mouths" ("*Salmonella* Bacteria...," 2007).

When this statement by the ARAV is compared with the injunctions in Leviticus 11:32-47, the astounding accuracy of the Old Testament regulation is again confirmed.

> Anything on which any of them falls, when they are dead shall be unclean, whether it is any item of wood or clothing or skin or sack, whatever item it is, in which any work is done, it must be put in water. And it shall be unclean until evening; then it shall be clean. Any earthen vessel into which any of them falls you shall break; and whatever is in it shall be unclean: in such a vessel, any edible food upon which water falls becomes unclean, and any drink that may be drunk from it becomes unclean (Leviticus 11:32-34).

After reading Leviticus 11:32-34, it seems as though a microbiologist was present with Moses to explain the perfect procedures to avoid spreading *Salmonella* and other bacteria from reptiles to humans. How could Moses have accurately laid down such precise regulations that belie a superior understanding of bacteria? An honest reader must conclude that he had divine assistance.

Bats and Rabies

Moses specifically forbade the Israelites to eat bats (Leviticus 11:19). The wisdom of this instruction is demonstrated by the fact that bats often carry rabies. While it is true that many animals are susceptible to rabies, bats are especially so. The American College of Emergency Physicians documented that between 1992 and 2002, rabies passed from bats caused 24 of the 26 human deaths from rabies in the United States ("Human Rabies...," 2002). In the *Science Daily* article describing this research, "Robert V. Gibbons, MD, MPH, of Walter Reed Army Institute of Research in Silver Spring, MD, reviewed the 24 cases of humans with bat rabies." From his research, he advised "the public to seek emergency care for preventive treatment for rabies **if direct contact with a bat occurs**" ("Human Rabies...," 2002). Moses' instruction to avoid bats coincides perfectly with modern research. Once again, the super-human wisdom imparted through Moses by God cannot be denied by the conscientious student of the Old Testament. As the eminent archaeologist, W.F. Albright, in comparing the list of clean and unclean animals detailed in the Pentateuch, noted that in other ancient civilizations, "we find no classifications as logical as this in any of the elaborate cuneiform list of fauna or ritual taboos" (1968, p. 180).

Case in Point: Pork Consumption

One of the most well-known Old Testament food regulations is the prohibition of pork consumption (Leviticus 11:7). Under close scrutiny, this prohibition exemplifies the value of the biblical laws regarding clean and unclean animals. During the days of Moses, proper food preparation and cooking conditions did not always exist. In fact, the general knowledge of the need to separate certain uncooked foods, especially meats, during preparation from other foods was virtually non-existent. Certain meats, if contacted raw or under-cooked, have greater potential to carry parasites and other harmful bacteria that can infect the end consumer (in this case, humans).

Due to the fact that pigs are scavengers, and will eat practically anything, they often consume parasites and bacteria when they eat the carcasses of other dead animals. These parasites and bacteria can, and often do, take up residence in the pigs' muscle tissue. Fully cooking the meat can kill these harmful organisms, but failure to cook the meat completely can cause numerous detrimental effects. R.K. Harrison listed several diseases or other health maladies that can occur due to the ingestion of improperly cooked pork. He noted that pigs often are the host of the tapeworm *Taenia solium*. Infection by this parasite can cause small tumors to arise throughout the body, including on the skin, eyes, and muscles. Furthermore, these tumors can affect the brain and cause epileptic convulsions. Additionally, humans can develop trichaniasis (*trichinosis*) infestation from eating undercooked, as well as tape worm known as *Echiococcus granulosus* from water polluted by pigs.

Further, pigs can pass on the microorganisms that cause toxoplamosis, a disease affecting the nervous system (Harrison, 1982, p. 644).

Due to a much more exhaustive body of knowledge concerning parasites and pathogens, modern readers are increasingly attune to the dangers of consuming raw or undercooked pork. In fact, most pork bought in grocery stores contains nitrates and nitrites that have been injected into the meat to hinder the growth of harmful microorganisms. But Moses and the Israelites did not have access to such modern knowledge. How is it that the food regulations recorded by Moses over 3,000 years ago contain such an accurate understanding of disease control? Albright noted along these lines, "thanks to the dietary and hygienic regulations of Mosaic law...subsequent history has been marked by a tremendous advantage in this respect held by Jews over all other comparable ethnic and religious groups" (1968, p. 181).

Circumcision

In the book of Genesis, the text relates that God chose Abraham and his descendants to be a "special" people who were set apart from all other nations. The covenant that God made with Abraham included a physical "sign" that was to be implemented in all future generations of Abraham's descendants. According to the text, God said:

> He who is eight days old among you shall be cir-
> cumcised, every male child in your generations, he
> who is born in your house or bought with money
> from any foreigner who is not your descendant. He
> who is born in your house and he who is bought

with your money must be circumcised, and My covenant shall be in your flesh for an everlasting covenant. And the uncircumcised male child, who is not circumcised in the flesh of his foreskin, that person shall be cut off from his people; he has broken My covenant (Genesis 17:12-14).

Thus, the covenant with Abraham and his offspring was to be indelibly marked in the flesh of every male child.

The inclusion of this medical, surgical practice provides another excellent example of the medical acumen of the biblical text. Two significant aspects of biblical circumcision need to be noted. First, from what modern medicine has been able to gather, circumcision can lessen the chances of getting certain diseases and infections. Pediatrician, Dorothy Greenbaum noted in regard to the health benefits of circumcision: "Medically, circumcision is healthful because it substantially reduces the incidence of urinary tract infection in boys, especially those under one year of age. Some studies cited in the pediatric policy statement report 10 to 20 times more urinary tract infection in uncircumcised compared with circumcised boys." She further noted that sexually transmitted diseases are passed more readily among men who have not been circumcised (2006). In addition, circumcision virtually eliminates the chance of penile cancer. In an article titled "Benefits of Circumcision," the text stated: "Neonatal circumcision virtually abolishes the risk [of penile cancer–KB]" and "penile cancer occurs almost entirely in uncircumcised men" (Morris, 2006). [NOTE: Morris' work is of particular interest due to the fact that it has an evolutionary bias and was in no way written to buttress belief in the biblical record.]

Not only can a litany of health benefits be amassed to encourage the practice of infant circumcision, but the day on which the biblical record commands the practice to be implemented is of extreme importance as well. The encyclopedic work *Holt Pediatrics* remains today one of the most influential works ever written about child care, pediatric disease, and other health concerns as they relate to children. First written in 1896 by L. Emmet Holt, Jr. and going through several revisions until the year 1953, the nearly 1,500-page work is a master compilation of the "modern" medicine of its day. One section, starting on page 125 of the twelfth edition, is titled "Hemorrhagic Disease of the Newborn." The information included in the section details the occurrence of occasional spontaneous bleeding among newborns that can sometimes cause severe damage to major organs such as the brain, and even death. In the discussion pertaining to the reasons for such bleeding, the authors note that the excessive bleeding is primarily caused by a decreased level of prothrombin, which in turn is caused by insufficient levels of vitamin K. The text also notes that children's susceptibility is "peculiar" (meaning "higher") "between the second and fifth days of life" (1953, p. 126).

In chart form, *Holt Pediatrics* illustrates that the percent of available prothrombin in a newborn dips from about 90% of normal on its day of birth to about 35% on its third day of life outside the womb. After the third day, the available prothrombin begins to climb. By the eighth day of the child's life, the available prothrombin level is approximately 110% of normal, about 20% higher than it was on the first day, and about 10% more than it will be during of the child's life. Such data prove that the eighth day is the perfect day on which to perform a major surgery such as circumcision.

How did Moses know such detailed data about newborn hemorrhaging? Some have suggested that the early Hebrews carried out extensive observations on newborns to determine the perfect day for surgery. But such an idea has little merit. McMillen and Stern noted:

> Modern medical textbooks sometimes suggest that the Hebrews conducted careful observations of bleeding tendencies. Yet what is the evidence? Severe bleeding occurs at most in only 1 out of 200 babies. Determining the safest day for circumcision would have required careful experiments, observing thousands of circumcisions. Could Abraham (a primitive, desert-dwelling nomad) have done that (2000, p. 84)?

In fact, such amazing medical accuracy cannot be accounted for on the basis of human ingenuity in the ancient world. If circumcision was the only example of such accuracy, and the Hebrew writings were laced with incorrect, detrimental medical prescriptions, such an explanation might be plausible. But the fact that the entire Old Testament contains medical practices that would still be useful in third world countries, without a hint of error in regard to a single prescription; divine oversight remains the only reasonable answer.

CONCLUSION

In reality, entire books could be written on the Old Testament's amazing medical accuracy. Medical doctors McMillen and Stern have done just that in their extremely interesting volume *None of These Diseases.* Many physicians who have compared Moses' medical instructions to effective modern methods have come to realize the astonishing value and insight of the Old Testament text. As Dr. Macht once wrote: "Every word in the Hebrew Scriptures is well chosen and carries valuable knowledge and deep significance" (Macht, 1953, p. 450). Such is certainly the case in regard to the medical practices listed in its pages. Indeed, the accurate medical practices prescribed thousands of years before their significance was completely understood provide excellent evidence for the divine inspiration of the Bible.

CHAPTER 8

BABYLON: A TEST CASE IN PROPHECY

by Wayne Jackson, M.A.[*]

It was the most remarkable community of its day—a San Francisco, New York, or London of the antique world. Herodotus (484-425 B.C.), known as the father of ancient history, once visited the great metropolis. He said that "in magnificence there is no other city that approaches to it" (1.178). It was Babylon!

Babylon's roots reached back almost to the dawn of civilization. Its genesis was with the mighty hunter, Nimrod, who conquered men and made them his unwilling subjects (Genesis 10:10). From that ignoble origin eventually evolved the Neo-Babylonian empire (614-539 B.C.), which figures so prominently in Old Testament history.

THE GOLDEN CITY

The city of Babylon straddled the Euphrates River about fifty miles south of what is now modern Baghdad in Iraq. Herodotus claimed that the town was laid out in an exact square, approximately fifteen miles on each side. The historian suggested that the city was

---

[*] Used with permission from: Wayne Jackson (1997), "Babylon, A Test Case in Prophecy," *Jeremiah & Lamentations* (Stockton, CA: Courier Publications).

surrounded by a moat (more than 260 feet broad), behind which was a massive wall—some 75 feet thick and
300 feet high, with 15 large gates of brass on each side.
Later writers (e.g., Strabo and Diodorus Siculus) gave
somewhat smaller dimensions. But these may reflect
different areas of measurement, or perhaps other historical periods (Keith, 1840, p. 271). When Jacob Abbott
wrote his fascinating volume, *History of Cyrus the Great*,
he suggested that Babylon was four or five times the
size of London (1850, p. 190). Modern archaeological
investigations have involved a significantly smaller area.
One of the prominent features of this illustrious city was
Nebuchadnezzar's Hanging Gardens, constructed for
his Median wife who was homesick for her hill-country
environment. This botanical marvel was considered
one of the seven wonders of the ancient world.

The Scriptures take note of the fame that characterized this community. The prophets designated Babylon
as "great" (Daniel 4:30), the "glory of the kingdoms"
(Isaiah 13:19), the "golden city" (Isaiah 14:4), the "lady
of the kingdoms" (Isaiah 47:5) who was "abundant in
treasures" (Jeremiah 51:13), and the "praise of the
whole earth" (Jeremiah 51:41). Surely a kingdom of
this nature could last forever.

BABYLON: THE INSTRUMENT
OF PROVIDENCE

In order to appreciate the significance of Babylon in
light of Bible prophecy, one must understand something
of Hebrew history. The northern kingdom of Israel
had been destroyed by the Assyrians in 722-721 B.C.
The southern kingdom (Judah) had been spared that

catastrophe (see Isaiah 37) but, due to her progressive apostasy, was on a clear collision course with Babylon. The prophets warned that if Judah continued her rebellion, Jehovah would raise up Nebuchadnezzar as His "servant" to punish the wayward Hebrews. Many of them would be killed; others would be captured and taken away as prisoners by the marauding Babylonians (Jeremiah 25:9). The Chaldean monarch, however, would not be commended or rewarded for this endeavor; rather, after his subjugation of Judah, the Lord would punish him, and the Babylon regime would commence a journey toward oblivion. Jeremiah summed up the history of this affair in the following way:

> Israel is a hunted sheep; the lions have driven him away: first, the king of Assyria devoured him; and now at last Nebuchadnezzar king of Babylon has broken his bones. Therefore thus says Jehovah of hosts, the God of Israel: Behold I will punish the king of Babylon and his land, as I have punished the king of Assyria (Jeremiah 50:17-18).

But Babylon was the epitome of arrogance. She boasted that no one would be able to conquer this powerful citadel. The Babylonians felt absolutely secure within their mighty fortress, and believed that the capital city would never be vanquished. "I shall be mistress forever.... I am, and there is none else besides me; I shall not sit as a widow, neither shall I know the loss of children" (Isaiah 47:7-8). Inscriptions from the Chaldean archives have illustrated the haughty disposition that characterized the Babylonian rulers (Millard, 1985, p. 138).

PROPHECY AS AN APOLOGETIC

Before I discuss prophecies relating to Babylon, there are some preliminary matters that must be considered. First, there is the nature of God—the eternal "I AM" (Exodus 3:14). He is the One Who is, Who was, and Who is to come (Revelation 1:4). He, and only He, knows the future as well as the past. The Lord, therefore, is able to speak of those things that "are not" as though "they were" (Romans 4:17).

Only God can know the future. If, then, we are able to establish the fact that the prophets announced—many years in advance—truths regarding the desolation of Babylon, it would amount to a demonstration that ultimately the biblical record was given by God Himself. These matters never could have been known by mere chance.

There is an interesting passage in the book of Jeremiah that illustrates this point. On a certain occasion in the prophet's ministry to Judah, Jeremiah was told by the Lord that his cousin, Hanamel, would arrive soon, offering to sell him a parcel of land in the town of Anathoth. Presently, Hanamel came to the prophet and made that very offer. Jeremiah subsequently uttered this significant statement: "**Then I knew** that this was the word of Jehovah" (Jeremiah 32:8, emp. added). When a prophecy is made—and the prediction comes to pass—one can **know** that God has spoken, provided other prophetic guidelines are in place.

PROPHETIC PRINCIPLES

In this chapter, we will survey some of the prophecies that focus upon Babylon's demise. First, though, let us remind ourselves of several principles that govern the validity of genuine prophecy. (1) True prophecies are stated emphatically; they are not couched in the jargon of contingency (unless, of course, contextual evidence suggests that one is dealing with a **conditional** prophecy). (2) Generally, a significant time frame must lapse between the prophetic utterance and the fulfillment, so as to exclude the possibility of "educated speculation." (3) The prophecy must involve specific details, not vague generalities. (4) The predictive declarations must be fulfilled precisely and completely. No mere substantial percentage will suffice. One should recognize, though, that occasionally a prophecy may contain figurative terminology; this does not, however, militate against its evidential validity.

In the forthcoming reflections, we will emphasize these important points: (1) Babylon's fall is announced unequivocally: (2) the time of the beginning of her end is declared; (3) the invading forces are specified; (4) particular details of the Chaldean destruction are chronicled; (5) the final result—Babylon's utter dissipation—is portrayed quite graphically. These factors, considered in concert, testify eloquently to the divine inspiration of the sacred Scriptures.

BABYLON TO FALL

In addition to the passage mentioned earlier (Jeremiah 50:17-18), there are many other prophecies that affirm the ultimate desolation of Babylon. In the early eighth century before the birth of Christ, and almost two hundred years before Cyrus conquered the "golden city," Isaiah declared: "Fallen, fallen is Babylon; and all the graven images of her gods are broken unto the ground" (21:9). The double use of "fallen" is for emphasis. Although the verb "fallen" is in the present tense form in English, it actually is in the perfect tense in Hebrew, which represents **completed** action. This reflects a grammatical idiom commonly known as the "prophetic perfect," frequently employed in the Old Testament to stress the absolute certainty of fulfillment (Freeman, 1968, pp. 122-123). The action thus is expressed confidently—as though it had been accomplished already.

Again Jehovah, through his prophet, rhetorically calls to Babylon: "Come down, and sit in the dust, O virgin daughter of Babylon; sit on the ground without a throne, O daughter of the Chaldeans" (Isaiah 47:1). Babylon is designated as a "virgin" because for many years she had escaped the ravages of other nations. But that status would come to an end!

Or consider the announcements of Jeremiah: "Declare you among the nations and publish, and set up a standard; publish, and conceal not: say, Babylon is taken" (Jeremiah 50:2). "Babylon is suddenly fallen and destroyed; wail for her; take balm for her pain" (Jeremiah 51:8). Among other contexts, a survey of Isaiah, chapters 13 and 14, and Jeremiah, chapters 50 and 51, will reveal numerous declarations concerning Babylon's impending fall and ultimate desolation.

THE PROPHETIC CHRONOLOGY

In giving consideration to the "time" factor in prophecies regarding the destruction of Babylon, two things must be kept in view. First, there was to be an

initial defeat of the superpower. Second, afterward there would be a **gradual but progressive degeneration** of the locale that ultimately would result in total ruin. At this point, we will consider only the first of these matters.

After Judah's good king, Josiah (639-608 B.C.), died during the battle of Megiddo, he was succeeded by his son Jehoahaz, a miserable failure who reigned only three months. Jehoahaz was taken captive to Egypt (2 Kings 23:30-34), where, as Jeremiah prophesied, he died (Jeremiah 22:11-12). Then Jehoiakim, Josiah's second son, came to Judah's throne. He reigned eleven years (608-597 B.C.). During his administration, the compassionate Jeremiah, via his prophetic proclamations, was attempting to bring the southern kingdom to a state of repentance—with little success, I might add. Let us focus momentarily upon the oracles of Jeremiah, chapter 25.

First, we must observe that the material of this important chapter is dated. "The word that came to Jeremiah concerning all the people of Judah, in the fourth year of Jehoiakim" (25:1). Thus, the following prophecies can be dated to 605 B.C. The prophet described the horrors that were to be visited upon Palestine by the impending Babylonian invasion. He then announced the fate of Babylon herself.

> And this whole land shall be a desolation, and an astonishment; and these nations [Judah and several of her neighbors—WJ] shall serve the king of Babylon seventy years. And it shall come to pass, when seventy years are accomplished, that I will punish the king of Babylon, and that nation, says Jehovah, for their iniquity (Jeremiah 25:11-12).

Thus, almost three-quarters of a century before Babylon fell, when there was absolutely no indication of Chaldean vulnerability, Jeremiah announced the impending doom of the ancient world's superpower, and he gave a time indicator as to when those circumstances would unfold. There simply was no natural way he could have "guessed" it.

THE CONQUERORS SPECIFIED

But who would overthrow mighty Babylon? Both Isaiah and Jeremiah provide that information. In a section that concludes with: "Fallen, fallen is Babylon," the messianic prophet wrote: "Go up, O Elam; besiege O Media; all the sighing thereof have I made to cease" (Isaiah 21:2). As I have noted elsewhere, "Elam is here used to facilitate the Hebrews' understanding of the source of the impending invasion, since Persia was not yet prominent. Later, Elam is considered as a part of the Persian empire..." (Jackson, 1991, p. 48). Skinner observed that Elam and Media were

> [t]he dominions of Cyrus. The former lay east of the Tigris and north of the Persian Gulf; Media was the mountainous district adjoining it on the north. Cyrus, according to the Babylonian records, was originally king of Anzan, in the north of Elam; in 549 he conquered Media, uniting the two in one kingdom (1963, 1:170).

Rawlinson noted that "Elam" is named because it was familiar to the Hebrews, whereas "Persia" would have been a designation alien to them at the time of Isaiah's writing (1950, 10:336). What precision!

Again, Isaiah detailed the conquering exploits of Cyrus, leader of the Medo-Persian forces and the brilliant strategist who overthrew the city of Babylon:

> Thus says Jehovah to his anointed, to Cyrus, whose right hand I have holden, to subdue nations before him, and I will loose the loins of kings; to open the doors before him, and the gates shall not be shut (45:1).

The prophecy was uttered two centuries before the birth of the Persian monarch, and yet, as I shall demonstrate subsequently, it set forth a number of remarkable events in connection with the conquest of the Chaldean capital.

Jeremiah was equally specific regarding the invaders of Babylon. "Make sharp the arrows, hold firm the shields: Jehovah has stirred up the spirit of the kings of the Medes; because his purpose is against Babylon to destroy it" (51:11). Some have suggested that this passage sarcastically urged the Babylonians to sharpen their arrows and firmly clutch their shields—as if they would be able to defend themselves against the Lord's forces (Clarke, n.d., 4:388). Others feel that this is a rhetorical charge to the Medo-Persian soldiers to prepare their military implements for attack against the Chaldean forces (Plumptre, 1959, 5:168). "The Persians were famous among the ancients for their archers" (McClintock and Strong, 1969, 1:372). Jehovah has plans for Babylon. He will destroy it by means of the "kings" (tribal rulers) of the Medes. Again, the accuracy of the biblical text is demonstrated by the precise terminology used. As Wiseman has noted concerning Jeremiah 51:11: "Babylonian texts (Nabonidus) show that the title

'king of the Medes' (11) was correctly in use in 544 B.C."
(Wiseman, 1979, p. 849).

The historical facts are not disputed. The Babylonian ruler, Nebuchadnezzar (605-562 B.C.), was
succeeded by his son, Evil-Merodach (562-560 B.C.),
who is mentioned in 2 Kings 25:27-30 and in Jeremiah
52:31-34. Next came Neriglissar (560-556 B.C.), an evil
conspirator who was defeated and slain in battle by
the Medes and Persians (Sanderson, et al., 1900, 1:54).
Labashi-Marduk subsequently came to the Chaldean
throne in 556 B.C., but was assassinated after a few
months. Finally, there was Nabonidus, who ruled
from 556-539 B.C. His son, Belshazzar, was co-regent
with his father. Actually it was Belshazzar who was
occupying the city of Babylon when it fell (see Daniel
5:1ff.). Inscriptions have been discovered which make
it clear that Nabonidus had entrusted the "kingship"
of the capital city to his son while he campaigned in
Arabia for about a decade (Vos, 1988, 1:276). When
Cyrus advanced against Babylon, Nabonidus marched
east to meet him, but fled before the Persian general's
army. Later, after Cyrus had captured the city (539
B.C.), Nabonidus surrendered to the Persians. And so,
the biblical prophecies regarding the conquerors of the
city of Babylon were fulfilled exactly.

BABYLON FEARFUL

The works of Herodotus and Xenophon are the two
principal sources of historical confirmation. Herodo
tus (484-425 B.C.), known as the "father of history,"
produced the first attempt at secular narrative history.
His work, which dealt primarily with the Persian Wars,

is an important source of information on the ancient world. He vividly describes the overthrow of Babylon. Xenophon (*circa* 430-355 B.C.), a student of Socrates, was a Greek historian born in Athens. He served in the Persian army and produced several valuable literary works. One of these, called *Cyropaedia*, is a sort of romance founded on the history of Cyrus the Great (559-530 B.C.). It provides considerable data on the fall of Babylon. Again, we emphasize that one of the traits of true prophecy is that it deals in **specific details**, not generalities. Let us examine some of these particulars.

Babylon had been a brutal force. She was "the glory of the kingdoms" (Isaiah 13:19). She had been Jehovah's providential "battle-axe" that had broken in pieces the nations of the ancient world (Jeremiah 51:20-24). For example, Nebuchadnezzar had defeated thoroughly the Egyptians at the battle of Carchemish (605 B.C.), and had enjoyed great success in Syria and Palestine, even subjugating "Zion" at the Lord's bidding.

One might surmise that Babylon would have feared no one. Oddly, though, Jeremiah said: "The mighty men of Babylon have ceased fighting. They stay in the strongholds; their strength is exhausted, they are becoming like women" (Jeremiah 51:30). How remarkably this conforms to the actual history. Xenophon said that when Cyrus brought his army to Babylon, he initially was perplexed as to how he would take the city, since the Chaldean soldiers "do not come out to fight" (VII. V.7). The Babylonians fearfully remained behind their massive walls refusing, for the most part, to encounter the enemy–exactly as the prophet had indicated.

EUPHRATES RIVER TO BE DIVERTED

When Cyrus surveyed Babylon's fortifications, he said: "I am unable to see how any enemy can take walls of such strength and height by assault" (Xenophon, VIII.V.7). Accordingly, he devised a brilliant strategy for capturing the city.

The Euphrates river ran under the walls through the center of Babylon. From the river, canals—quite broad and sometimes navigable—were cut in every direction. The Jews in captivity could thus lament: "By the rivers of Babylon, There we sat down, yea, we wept, When we remembered Zion" (Psalm 137:1). Just to the west of the city was a huge lake-basin, some thirty-five feet deep and covering forty miles square, but which, at the time of the invasion, was but a marsh. Cyrus stationed soldiers at the point where the river entered the city, and also where it exited. At a given time, he diverted the Euphrates from its bed into the marshy lake area. His forces then entered Babylon under the city walls (Herodotus, I.191).

Consider what the prophets declared regarding Babylon's fall. Isaiah, writing more than a century and a half earlier, referred to Jehovah's decree. The Lord "saith to the deep: Be dry, and I will dry up thy rivers, that saith of Cyrus, he is my shepherd and shall perform my pleasure" (Isaiah 47:27). Some contend that the language of this passage is an allusion to the Exodus, which occurred in Israel's early history. That cannot be the case, however. The utterance is framed in the future tense, and the context specifically relates this matter to Cyrus. The prophecy "is usually taken as referring to the device Cyrus used in order to capture Babylon" (Fitch, 1954, p. 593).

Later, in his famous oracle against Babylon, Jeremiah exclaimed: "A drought is upon her waters, and they shall be dried up: for it is a land of graven images, and they are mad over idols" (50:38). Again, "I will dry up her sea, and make her fountain dry" (51:36). Though these passages have been interpreted in various ways, the language is quite consistent with the diversion of the river, which allowed the Persians to take the city virtually unopposed (see Wiseman, 1979, p. 849).

SURPRISE CAPTURE DURING DRUNKEN FEAST

Concerning Babylon's fall, Jeremiah represented the Lord as saying: "I have laid a snare for you, and you are also taken, O Babylon" (50:24). The term "snare" suggests that the citizens of the city would be taken by surprise; they "were not aware" of what was happening until it was too late (50:24b). Herodotus wrote: "Had the Babylonians been apprised of what Cyrus was about, or had they noticed their danger, they would never have allowed the Persians to enter their city" (I.191).

One aspect in the rapid conquest of the city had to do with the fact that the Babylonians, in their smug security, were engaged in drunken festivities; thus, they were wholly unconcerned about the enemy beyond their massive walls. But the Lord had declared: "When they are heated, I will make their feast, and I will make them drunken, that they may rejoice, and sleep a perpetual sleep, and not wake, says Jehovah"

(Jeremiah 51:39). Again: "And I will make drunk her princes and her wise men, her governors and her deputies, and her mighty men; and they shall sleep a perpetual sleep, and not wake, says the King whose name is Jehovah of hosts" (Jeremiah 51:57).

Herodotus recorded that the citizens of the central section of the city did not know that Babylon had fallen for a good while because "they were engaged in a festival, continued dancing and reveling until they learnt the capture" (I.191). Similarly, Xenophon said that "there was a festival in Babylon, in which all the Babylonians drank and reveled the whole night" (VII.5.15).

BABYLON TO BE SACKED

The prophets indicated that when great Babylon was taken, her rich treasures would be looted. The Lord, speaking prophetically to Cyrus, had promised: "[A]nd I will give you the treasures of darkness, and hidden riches of secret places" (Isaiah 45:3). Jeremiah announced: "And they shall become as women: a sword is upon her treasures, and they shall be robbed" (50:37). The treasures of Babylon were splendid beyond description. Herodotus, in describing just one of the temples in the city, declared that it contained more than twenty tons of gold (I.183). It is interesting to note that when Cyrus issued his famous decree that allowed the Jews to return to their land, he endowed them with silver and gold to help finance the project, as well as returning some 5,400 vessels of gold and silver that originally had been taken from the Hebrew temple (Ezra 1:4,11).

When Jehovah beckoned the Persians to come against evil Babylon, He charged: "[O]pen up her store-houses [granaries, ASV footnote]; cast her up as heaps, and destroy her utterly; let nothing of her be left" (Jeremiah 50:26). Xenophon reports that Babylon "was furnished with provisions for more than twenty years" (VIII.5.13). No wonder they felt secure; the storehouses were bulging. But God emptied them—just as His prophet had announced!

WALLS TO BE ABOLISHED

I already have mentioned Babylon's famous walls. An ancient historian, Diodorus, stated that it took 200,000 men a full year to construct these fortifications (Fausset, 1990, 2[2]:181). But Jeremiah prophesied: "The broad walls of Babylon shall be utterly overthrown, and her high gates shall be burned with fire" (51:58). Where are Babylon's walls, and her one hundred gates of brass today? (Herodotus, I.179). Under the "Summary" below, I will detail more precisely the demolition of the city.

BABYLON TO FADE INTO OBLIVION

The prophets repeatedly proclaimed the eventual utter desolation of ancient Babylon. Isaiah gave the following particulars:

> And Babylon, the glory of kingdoms, the beauty of the Chaldeans' pride, shall be as when God overthrew Sodom and Gomorrah. It shall never be inhabited, neither shall it be dwelt in from generation to generation: neither shall the Arabian pitch tent there; neither shall shepherds make their flocks to lie down there. But wild beasts of the desert shall

live there; and their houses shall be full of doleful creatures; and ostriches shall dwell there, and wild goats shall dance there. And wolves shall cry in their castles, and jackals in the pleasant palaces: and her time is near to come, and her days shall not be prolonged (13:19-22).

Jeremiah was equally graphic; the reader may consult chapters 50 and 51 of his book for the numerous details given there.

At this point, I would like to mention two points. First, there was to be an **initial defeat** of Babylon. Second, afterwards there would be a **gradual but progressive degeneration** of the locale, which ultimately would become a site of absolute waste. In the following section, I will catalogue the destructions and degeneration of once-great Babylon.

A SUMMARY OF EVENTS

1. After a siege of two years, the city of Babylon was captured by Cyrus, commander of the Medo-Persian forces, in October of 539 B.C. This brought the Neo-Babylonian empire (614-539 B.C.) to a close. Significant damage to the city was not inflicted at this time, though some of the walls may have been broken down, at least partially.

2. Following a rebellion of the Babylonian subjects, Darius Hystaspes took the city again in 520 B.C. He demolished the walls significantly and carried off the huge gates (see Jeremiah 51:58). Elsewhere I have given a detailed account of how the city was taken—again by a "snare" (Jackson, 1996). Herodotus wrote: "Thus was Babylon taken for a second time. Darius having become master of the place, destroyed the wall, and tore down all the gates; for Cyrus had done neither the one nor the other when he took Babylon" (III.159). Ap-

parently, however, there was some subsequent repair of the walls (see McClintock and Strong, 1969, 1:596).

3. During the reign of Xerxes (485-465 B.C.), the temple of Bel (Marduk) was plundered and destroyed. Much of the city was turned into ruins in 483 B.C., and the walls were dismantled further.

4. Babylon again fell to Alexander the Great in 331 B.C. As Alexander neared the city, priests and nobles went out to meet him with lavish gifts, surrendering the city. Alexander proposed that he would rebuild the temple of Marduk. He employed 10,000 men to clear the dirt and rubble. They labored in vain for two months. Alexander died and the work was abandoned (Rollin, 1857, 1:575). A clay tablet has been found that confirms this enterprise. It records that in the sixth year of Alexander's reign, he made a payment of ten manehs of silver for "clearing away the dust of E-sagila [Marduk's great temple]" (King, 1919, 2:284-288).

5. In 270 B.C. Antiochus Soter, a Greek ruler, restored several of the temples in Babylon, but the general decay of the city continued.

6. In the time of Strabo (at the end of the 1st century B.C.), the site was in ruins. Jerome (fourth century A.D.), learned that Babylon had been used as a wild game park for the amusement of numerous Persian dignitaries (McClintock and Strong, 1969, 1:596). In the fifth century A.D., according to Cyril of Alexandria, due to the bursting of canal banks, Babylon became a swamp (Jeremias, 1911, 1:294).

7. Volney, the French atheist who was such a militant adversary of the Bible, wrote his book, *The Ruins of Empires*, in 1791. Therein he stated: "Nothing is left of Babylon but heaps of earth, trodden under foot of men" (as quoted in Holman, 1926, p. 333). As Jeremiah had prophesied: "[C]ast her up as heaps" (50:26). It is iron-

ic that a skeptic should lend support to confirming the accuracy of the biblical narrative!

8. When archaeologist Austen Layard explored Babylon in the mid-nineteenth century, he described the heaps of rubbish that rendered the area a "naked and hideous waste" (1856, p. 413). Later, when Robert Koldewey excavated the city for eighteen seasons beginning in 1899, he said that as he gazed over the ruins, he could not help but be reminded of Jeremiah 50:39 (1914, p. 314). He reported that many of the sites were covered with forty to eighty feet of sand and rubble.

9. A relatively modern air-view of Babylonia—once the world's greatest city—shows only a mound of dirt and broken-down walls (Boyd, 1969, pp. 153ff.).

In recent years, Saddam Hussein attempted to build a tourist center near the site of old Babylon. The 1990 Persian Gulf War seriously impaired his plans.

THE CRITICS AND THE PROPHECY

The accuracy of the dozens of prophecies regarding the fall of Babylon has baffled skeptics for generations. So remarkable has been the precision of the fulfillment that critics often have resorted to **redating** the predictions in both Isaiah and Jeremiah so as to make them appear to be records of **history** instead of **prophecy**! For example, in commenting upon the oracles of Jeremiah, chapters 50-51, James Philip Hyatt wrote: "Some of the poems in this present collection seem to reflect the city's downfall, as prophecies **after the event** rather than predictions..." (1956, 5:1124, emp. added). Such a view ignores the evidence for dating the books at a much earlier period.

A former professor in a Christian university has even capitulated to this liberal viewpoint. Anthony Ash asserted:

> Dating chapter 50 is virtually impossible. The arrangement of the text indicates that it was a composite, probably containing materials from different periods.... The chapter may have reached this form near the mid-sixth century B.C., when the fall of Babylon appeared likely (1987, p. 309, emp. added).

Upon this basis, then, one supposes that Jeremiah—or whoever put the composite together!—simply made a **lucky guess** as to the fall of Babylon. Such a view is disgusting, and unworthy of any Christian writer.

CONCLUSION

The prophetic details regarding the fall of ancient Babylon, as minutely recorded in the Old Testament narratives, truly are astounding. This is but another example of the amazing evidence that demonstrates the character of the Bible as the inspired Word of God.

CHAPTER 9

TYRE IN PROPHECY

Ezekiel's prophetic message is one of the simplest to place in an accurate time frame. In verse 2 of the first chapter, the prophet noted that his visions and prophecies began "in the fifth year of King Johoiachin's captivity." The date for this captivity is virtually unanimously accepted as 597 B.C., during the second deportation of citizens from Judea to Babylon, which is documented in detail in 2 Kings 24:10-20. Furthermore, not only is the deportation recorded in the biblical account, but the ancient Chaldean records document it as well (Free and Vos, 1992, p. 194). Since Ezekiel's visions began five years after the deportation, a firm date of 592 B.C. can be established for the beginning of his prophecy. The prophet supplies other specific dates such as the seventh year (20:1), the ninth year (24:1), the eleventh year (26:1), and the latest date given as the twenty-seventh year (29:17) [NOTE: for an outline see Archer, 1974, pp. 368-369].

Due to the firmly established dating system that Ezekiel chose to use for his prophecy, the date of the prophecy regarding the city of Tyre, found in chapter

26, can be accurately established as the eleventh year after 597, which would be 586 B.C.

THE CITY OF TYRE

According to history, the Phoenician city of Tyre, located on the eastern shore of the Mediterranean Sea, stood as one of the most ancient and prosperous cities in history. Herodotus lived and wrote between about 490 B.C. and 425 B.C. (Herodotus, 1972, p. i). During a visit to the temple of Heracles in Tyre, Herodotus inquired about the age of the temple, to which the inhabits replied that the temple was as old as "Tyre itself, and that Tyre had already stood for two thousand three hundred years" (Herodotus, 2.44). From Herodotus, then, it can be ascertained that the city supposedly can be traced back to 2,700 B.C.

Due to its advantageous geographical position and good ports, Tyre became one of the wealthiest trading cities in history. Fleming noted that it "was the most important of all Phoenician cities" (1966, p. ix). During the reigns of King David and King Solomon (*circa* 1000 B.C.), Hiram, king of Tyre, played a major role in the acquisition of building materials for important structures such as the Israelite kings' houses and the first temple. In numerous biblical passages, the text states that Hiram sent cedar trees, carpenters, masons, and builders to Israel (2 Samuel 5:11) because of the Tyrians' renowned skill in timber cutting (1 Kings 5:1-18). In addition, the Tyrians were equally well known for their remarkable abilities to navigate the seas during Solomon's era. Second Chronicles documents that Hiram sent ships and "servants who knew the sea" to work with Solomon's men in acquiring gold from foreign lands (1 Kings 8:18).

The city of Tyre had a rather interesting and beneficial geographical arrangement. About half a mile off the eastern shore of the Mediterranean Sea stood a small rocky island on which the original city of Tyre was most likely founded. Some time after the founding of this island city, the mainland city of Tyre, which the Greeks called "Old Tyre," was founded (Fleming, 1966, p. 4). Josephus cites a Phoenician historian named Dius, as reporting that the Phoenician king Hiram, who was closely connected to kings David and Solomon, built a causeway from the original island to a smaller island, connecting the two (*Against Apion*, 1.17).

In addition to its beneficial geographic position, the city had great confidence in its many excellent defensive advantages. Fleming noted: "As early as 1400 B.C. Tyre was not only a great city but was considered impregnable" (1966, p. 8). The ancient historian Quintus Curtius Rufus (most likely writing in approximately A.D. 50), listed several of these defensive traits that had remained intact as late as the siege by Alexander in 332 B.C. The force of the water and the wind that prevailed on the side of the city closest to the land was said to have produced a "corrosive force of waves" that would hinder the construction of any type of bridge or causeway from the mainland (4.2.8). Furthermore, the water nearest to the walls of the city was "especially deep" and would force any would-be attackers to position any type of siege mechanisms in the unstable foundation of a ship, and the wall "dropped sheer into the sea," which prevented the use of ladders or approach by foot (4.2.9).

During the time of Ezekiel, Tyre was well established and renowned for its building, manufacturing, and trade. Ezekiel said of Tyre: "Your builders have perfected your beauty" (27:4), and then he proceeded to list several different kinds of wood and imported materials used by the Tyrians (27:3-11). The prophet stated: "When your wares went out by sea, you satisfied many people; you enriched the kings of the earth with your many luxury goods and your merchandise" (27:33).

But Tyre's profitable trading had done little to improve its spiritual condition. In fact, as is often the case, the riches accrued by the city had caused widespread dereliction and spiritual decay. Concerning the city, Ezekiel noted: "By the abundance of your trading you became filled with violence within, and you sinned.... Your heart was lifted up because of your beauty; you corrupted your wisdom for the sake of splendor.... You defiled your sanctuaries by the multitude of your iniquities" (28:16-18). Among the sins listed by Ezekiel, one specific attitude maintained by Tyre was designated by the prophet as the ultimate reason for the city's demise. Ezekiel noted: "[B]ecause Tyre has said against Jerusalem, 'Aha! She is broken who was the gateway of the peoples; now she is turned over to me; I shall be filled; she is laid waste.' Therefore thus says the Lord God: 'Behold, I am against you, O Tyre'" (26:2-3). Apparently, in an attitude of commercial jealousy and greed, the city of Tyre exulted in Jerusalem's misfortunes and expected to turn them into its own profit. Among Tyre's list of despicable activities, the city's slave trade ranked as one of the most profitable. The prophet Joel noted that Tyre had taken the people from Judah and

Jerusalem and sold them to the Greeks so that the Tyrians could "remove them far from their borders" (Joel 3:6). These dastardly dealings with the inhabitants of Judah would not go unpunished.

In Ezekiel 26, the prophet mentioned several events that were to occur in Tyre as punishment for the city's arrogance and merciless actions. The following is a lengthy, but necessary, quote from that chapter:

> Therefore thus says the Lord God: "Behold, I am against you, O Tyre, and will cause many nations to come up against you, as the sea causes its waves to come up. And they shall destroy the walls of Tyre and break down her towers; I will also scrape her dust from her, and make her like the top of a rock. It shall be a place for spreading nets in the midst of the sea, for I have spoken," says the Lord God; "it shall become plunder for the nations. Also her daughter villages which are in the fields shall be slain by the sword. Then they shall know that I am the Lord."
>
> For thus says the Lord God: "Behold, I will bring against Tyre from the north Nebuchadnezzar king of Babylon, king of kings, with horses, with chariots, and with horsemen, and an army with many people. He will slay with the sword your daughter villages in the fields; he will heap up a siege mound against you, build a wall against you, and raise a defense against you. He will direct his battering rams against your walls, and with his axes he will break down your towers. Because of the abundance of his horses, their dust will cover you; your walls will shake at the noise of the horsemen, the wagons, and the chariots, when he enters your gates, as men enter a city that has been breached. With the hooves of his horses he will

trample all your streets; he will slay your people by the sword, and your strong pillars will fall to the ground. They will plunder your riches and pillage your merchandise; they will break down your walls and destroy your pleasant houses; they will lay your stones, your timber, and your soil in the midst of the water. I will put an end to the sound of your songs, and the sound of your harps shall be heard no more. I will make you like the top of a rock; you shall be a place for spreading nets, and you shall never be rebuilt, for I the Lord have spoken," says the Lord God....

For thus says the Lord God: "When I make you a desolate city, like cities that are not inhabited, when I bring the deep upon you, and great waters cover you, then I will bring you down with those who descend into the Pit, to the people of old, and I will make you dwell in the lowest part of the earth, in places desolate from antiquity, with those who go down to the Pit, so that you may never be inhabited; and I shall establish glory in the land of the living. I will make you a terror, and you shall be no more; though you are sought for, you will never be found again," says the Lord God (26:1-21).

Several aspects of this prophecy deserve attention and close scrutiny. The prophet predicted: (1) many nations would come against Tyre; (2) the inhabitants of the villages and fields of Tyre would be slain; (3) Nebuchadnezzar would build a siege mound against the city; (4) the city would be broken down and the stones, timber, and soil would be thrown in "the midst of the water;" (5) the city would become a "place for spreading nets;" and (6) the city would never be rebuilt.

In chronological order, the siege of Nebuchadnezzar took place within a few months of Ezekiel's prophecy. Josephus, quoting "the records of the Phoenicians," says that Nebuchadnezzar "besieged Tyre for thirteen years in the days of Ithobal, their king" (*Against Apion*, 1.21). The length of the siege was due, in part, to the unusual arrangement of the mainland city and the island city. While the mainland city would have been susceptible to ordinary siege tactics, the island city would have been easily defended against orthodox siege methods (Fleming, 1966, p. 45). The historical record suggests that Nebuchadnezzar destroyed the mainland city, but the siege of the island "probably ended with the nominal submission of the city" in which Tyre surrendered "without receiving the hostile army within her walls" (p. 45). The city of Tyre was besieged by Nebuchadnezzar, who did major damage to the mainland as Ezekiel predicted, but the island city remained primarily unaffected.

It is at this point in the discussion that certain skeptics view Ezekiel's prophecy as a failed prediction. Farrell Till stated: "Nebuchadnezzar did capture the mainland suburb of Tyre, but he never succeeded in taking the island part, which was the seat of Tyrian grandeur. That being so, it could hardly be said that Nebuchadnezzar wreaked the total havoc on Tyre that Ezekiel vituperatively predicted in the passages cited" (n.d.). Till and others suggest that the prophecies about Tyre's utter destruction refer to the work of Nebuchadnezzar.

After a closer look at the text, however, such an interpretation is misguided. Ezekiel began his prophecy by stating that "many nations" would come against Tyre

(26:3). Then he proceeded to name Nebuchadnezzar, and stated that "he" would build a siege mound, "he" would slay with the sword, and numerous other things that "he" would do (26:7-11). However, in 26:12, the pronoun shifts from the singular "he" to the plural "they." It is in verse twelve and following that Ezekiel predicts that "they" will lay the stones and building material of Tyre in the "midst of the waters." The shift in pronouns is of vast significance, since it shifts the subject of the action from Nebuchadnezzar (he) back to the many nations (they). Till and others fail to see this shift and mistakenly apply the utter destruction of Tyre to the efforts of Nebuchadnezzar.

Furthermore, Ezekiel was well aware of Nebuchadnezzar's failure to destroy the city. Sixteen years after his initial prediction, in the 27th year of Johoiachin's captivity (*circa* 570 B.C.), he wrote: "Son of man, Nebuchadnezzar king of Babylon caused his army to labor strenuously against Tyre; every head was made bald, and every shoulder rubbed raw; yet neither he nor his army received wages from Tyre, for the labor which they expended on it" (29:18). Therefore, in regard to the prophecy of Tyre as it relates to Nebuchadnezzar's activity at least two of the elements were fulfilled (i.e., the siege mound and the slaying of the inhabitants in the field).

Regarding the prediction that "many nations" would come against Tyre, the historical records surrounding the illustrious city report such turmoil and war that Ezekiel's prophecy looks like a mild understatement of the facts. After Nebuchadnezzar's attack, "a period of great depression" plagued the city, which was assimilated into the Persian Empire around 538 B.C. (Fleming, 1966, p. 47). In 392 B.C., "Tyre was involved in the war which arose between the Persians and Evagorus of Cyprus" in which the king of Egypt "took Tyre by assault" (p. 52). Sixty years later, in 332, Alexander the Great besieged Tyre and crushed it (see below for further elaboration). Soon after this defeat, Ptolemy of Egypt conquered and subjugated Tyre until about 315 B.C. when Atigonus of Syria besieged Tyre for 15 months and captured it (Fleming, p. 65). In fact, Tyre was contested by so many foreign forces that Fleming wrote: "It seemed ever the fate of the Phoenician cities to be between an upper and a nether millstone" (p. 66). Babylon, Syria, Egypt, Rome, Greece, Armenia, and Persia are but a sampling of the "many nations" that had a part in the ultimate destruction of Tyre. Thus, Ezekiel's prophecy about "many nations" remains as a historical reality that cannot be gainsaid.

ALEXANDER AND TYRE

The historical account of Alexander the Great's dealings with Tyre adds another important piece to Ezekiel's prophecy. By 333 B.C., Ezekiel's prophecy that Tyre would be destroyed and its building material cast into the midst of the waters had yet to materialize. But that situation was soon to be altered. Ancient historian Diodorus Siculus, who lived from approximately 80-20 B.C., wrote extensively of the young Greek conqueror's dealing with Tyre. It is from his original work that much of the following information on Tyre's destruction derives (see Siculus, 17.40-46).

In his dealings with Tyre, Alexander asserted that he wished to make a personal sacrifice in the temple of Heracles on the island city of Tyre. Apparently, because the Tyrians considered their island refuge virtually impregnable, with war machines covering the walls, and rapidly moving water acting as an effective barrier from land attack, they refused his request. Upon receiving their refusal, Alexander immediately set to work on a plan to besiege and conquer the city. He started building a land bridge or causeway (Siculus calls it a "mole") from the mainland city of Tyre to the island city. Siculus stated: "Immediately he demolished what was called Old Tyre and set many tens of thousands of men to work carrying stones to construct a mole" (17.40). Curtius Rufus noted: "Large quantities of rock were available, furnished by old Tyre" (4.2.18). This unprecedented action took the Tyrians by complete surprise. Fleming noted: "In former times the city had shown herself well nigh impregnable. That Alexander's method of attack was not anticipated is not strange, for there was no precedent for it in the annals of warfare" (1966, p. 56). And yet, even though this action was unprecedented militarily, it was exactly what one might expect from the description of the destruction of Tyre given by Ezekiel hundreds of years prior to Alexander's actions. The mainland city was demolished and all her stones, timber, and soil were thrown into the midst of the sea.

In spite of the fact that the Tyrians were taken by surprise, they were not disheartened, because they did not believe that Alexander's efforts would prevail. They continued to maintain supremacy on the sea, and harassed his workers from all sides from boats that were equipped with catapults, slingers, and archers. These tactics were effective in killing many of Alexander's men. But Alexander was not to be outdone. He gathered his own fleet of ships from nearby cities and was successful in neutralizing the Tyrian vessels' effectiveness.

With the arrival of Alexander's sea fleet, the work on the land bridge moved much more rapidly. Yet, when the construction of the bridge was nearing completion, a storm damaged a large section of the mole. Refusing to quit, Alexander rebuilt the damaged structure and continued to move forward. In desperation, the Tyrians sent underwater divers to impede construction by attaching hooks to the rocks and trees of the causeway, causing much damage (Rufus, 4.3.10). Yet, these efforts by the Tyrians could not stop Alexander's army, and eventually the bridge spanned the distance from the mainland city to the island. Huge siege machines bombarded the walls of Tyre. Siculus' description of the fight is one of the most vivid accounts of a battle in ancient history (17.43-46). Eventually the Tyrians were defeated, their walls penetrated, and Alexander's forces entered the city and devastated it. Most of the men of Tyre were killed in continued fighting. Siculus recorded that approximately 2,000 of the men in Tyre who were of military age were crucified, and about 13,000 "non-combatants" were sold into slavery (17.46) [Others estimate the number even higher.] In describing the devastation of the city by Alexander, Fleming wrote: "There was general slaughter in the streets and square. The Macedonians were enraged by the stubborn resistance of the city and especially by the recent murder of some of their countrymen; they therefore showed no mercy. A large part of the city was burned" (p. 63).

The secular historical record detailing Alexander's destruction of Tyre coincides precisely with Ezekiel's prophecy concerning what would happen to its building materials. As Ezekiel had predicted, the stones, timber, and soil of the mainland city were thrown into the midst of the sea in an unprecedented military venture. For Ezekiel to have accurately "guessed" this situation would be to stretch the law of probability beyond the limits of absurdity. His acutely accurate representation of the facts remains as outstanding and amazing proof of the divine inspiration behind his message.

ADDITIONAL ASPECTS OF
THE PROPHECY OF TYRE

One of the most disputed aspects concerning Eze-kiel's prophecy is the statement that the city of Tyre would "never be rebuilt" (26:14), and "be no more forever" (28:19). The skeptic points to modern day Tyre and suggests that these statements have failed to materialize. Till stated: "In fact, Tyre still exists today, as anyone able to read a map can verify. This obvious failure of a highly touted Old Testament prophet is just one more nail in the coffin of the Bible inerrancy doctrine" (n.d.).

Several possible solutions exist that dissolve this alleged problem. First, it could be the case that the bulk of Ezekiel's prophecy dealt with the mainland city of Tyre, the location of which has most likely been lost permanently and is buried under the waters of the Mediterranean Sea. This solution has merit for several reasons. In approximately A.D. 1170, a Jewish traveler named Benjamin of Tudela published a diary of his travels. "Benjamin began his journey from Saragossa, around the year 1160 and over the course of thirteen years visited over 300 cities in a wide range of places including Greece, Syria, Palestine, Mesopotamia and Persia" (Benjamin of Tudela, n.d.). In his memoirs, a section is included concerning the city of Tyre.

> From Sidon it is half a day's journey to Sarepta (Sarfend), which belongs to Sidon. Thence it is a half-day to New Tyre (Sur), which is a very fine city, with a harbour in its midst.... There is no harbour like this in the whole world. Tyre is a beautiful city.... In the vicinity is found sugar of a high class, for men plant it here, and people come from all lands to buy it. A man can ascend the walls of New Tyre **and see ancient Tyre, which the sea has now covered**, lying at a stone's throw from the new city. And should one care to go forth by boat, one can see the castles, market-places, streets, and palaces **in the bed of the sea** (1907, emp. added.).

From this twelfth-century A.D. text, then, we learn that by that period of time the city known as ancient Tyre lay completely buried beneath the sea and a new city, most likely on some part of the island, had been erected. George Davis, in his book *Fulfilled Prophecies that Prove the Bible*, included a picture of Syrian fishermen under which the following caption appeared: "Syrian fishermen hauling in their nets on the probable site of ancient Tyre, which perished as predicted by the prophet" (1931, p. 11). In his monumental work on the city of Tyre, Katzenstein mentioned several ancient sources that discussed the position of "Old Tyre." He wrote: "Later this town was dismantled by Alexander the Great in his famous siege of Tyre and **disappeared totally with the change of the coastline** brought about by the dike and the alluvial deposits that changed Tyre into a peninsula" (1973, p. 15, emp. added).

It very likely is the case that the specific site of ancient Tyre has been buried by sand and water over the course of the last 2,500 years and is lost to modern knowledge. That the prophet was speaking about the mainland city in reference to many aspects of his prophecy has much to commend it. It was to that mainland city that King Nebuchadnezzar directed most of his attention and destructive measures described in Ezekiel 26:8-11. Furthermore, it was the mainland city that Alexander destroyed completely and cast into the sea to build his causeway to the island city. In addition, Benjamin Tudela's quote corresponds precisely to the statement that the prophet made in the latter part of chapter 26: "For thus says the Lord God: 'When I make you a desolate city, like the cities that are not inhabited, **when I bring the deep upon you, and great waters cover you**'" (26:19, emp. added). In addition, Katzenstein noted that the scholar H.L. Ginsberg has suggested that the name "Great Tyre" was given to the mainland city, while the island city was designated as "Little Tyre" (p. 20). He further noted 2 Samuel 24:7, which mentions "the stronghold of Tyre," and commented that this "may refer to "Old Tyre," or the mainland city (p. 20).

Besides the idea that the bulk of the prophecy dealt with the mainland city, other possible solutions exist that sufficiently support the prediction that Tyre would "never be rebuilt" and would "be no more forever." While it is true that a city does currently exist on the island, that city is not a "rebuilt" Tyre and has no real connection to the city condemned by Ezekiel other than its location. If the history of Tyre is traced more completely, it becomes evident that even the island city of Tyre suffered complete destruction. Fleming noted that in approximately A.D. 193: "Tyre was plundered and burned after a fearful slaughter of her citizens" (1966, p. 73). Around the year 1085, the Egyptians "succeeded in reducing Tyre, which for many years had been practically independent" (p. 85). Again, in about 1098, the Vizier of Egypt "entered the city and massacred a large number of people" (p. 88). In addition, the city was besieged in A.D. 1111 (p. 90), and again in April of 1124 (p. 95). Around the year 1155, the Egyptians entered Tyre, "made a raid with fire and sword...and carried off many prisoners and much plunder" (p. 101).

In addition to the military campaigns against the city, at least two major earthquakes pummeled the city, one of which "ruined the wall surrounding the city" (p. 115). And ultimately, in A.D. 1291, the Sultan Halil massacred the inhabitants of Tyre and subjected the city to utter ruin. "Houses, factories, temples, everything in the city was consigned to the sword, flame and ruin" (p. 122). After this major defeat in 1291, Fleming cites several travel logs in which visitors to the city mention that citizens of the area in 1697 were "only a few poor wretches...subsisting chiefly upon fishing" (p. 124). In 1837, another earthquake pounded the remains of the city so that the streets were filled with debris from fallen houses to such a degree that they were impassable (p. 128).

Taking these events into consideration, it is obvious that many nations continued to come against the island city, that it was destroyed on numerous occasions, and that it became a place for fishing, fulfilling Ezekiel's prediction about the spreading of nets. Furthermore, it is evident that the multitudinous periods of destruction and rebuilding of the city have long since buried the Phoenician city that came under the condemnation of Ezekiel. The *Columbia Encyclopedia*, under its entry for Tyre, noted: "The principal ruins of the city today are those of buildings erected by the Crusaders. There are some Greco-Roman remains, but **any left by the Phoenicians lie underneath the present town**" ("Tyre," 2006, emp. added). Concerning Tyre's present condition, other sources have noted that "continuous settlement has restricted excavation to the Byzantine and Roman levels **and information about the Phoenician town** comes only from documentary sources" ("Ancient Tyre...," n.d., emp. added). Another report confirmed, "Uncovered remains are from the post-Phoenician Greco-Roman, Crusader, Arab and Byzantine times.... **Any traces of the Phoenician city** were either destroyed long ago or remain buried under today's city" ("Ancient Phoenicia," n.d., emp. added). Thus, the only connection that the present town maintains with the ancient one in Ezekiel's day is location, and the present buildings, streets, and other features are not "rebuilt" versions of the original city. If Ezekiel's prophecy extended to the island city as well as the mainland city, it can be maintained legitimately that the ruins lying underneath the city have not been "rebuilt."

WHEN DID EZEKIEL PROPHESY?

Some have questioned the date of the composition of Ezekiel, due to the prophecy's amazing accuracy in regard to its predictions concerning Tyre. Yet, the book of Ezekiel has much that lends itself to the idea that it was composed by Ezekiel during the time it claims to have been written. When did Ezekiel write his material? Kenny Barfield noted that, besides a belief that supernatural revelation is impossible,

> no evidence supports the thesis that Ezekiel's predictions were penned later than 400 B.C. Moreover, the book (Ezek. 1:1; 8:1; 33:1; 40:1-4) claims to have been composed by the prophet sometime in the sixth century, B.C., and Josephus attributes the book to the Hebrew prophet during the time in question (1995, p. 98).

In addition, Ezekiel was included in the Septuagint, which is the "earliest version of the Old Testament Scriptures" available—a translation from Hebrew to Greek which was "executed at Alexandria in the third century before the Christian era" (*Septuagint,* 1998, p. i).

Simon Greenleaf, the lawyer who is renowned for having played a major role in the founding of Harvard Law School and for having written the *Treatise on the Law of Evidence,* scrutinized several biblical documents in light of the procedures practiced in a court of law. He noted one of the primary laws regarding ancient documents: "Every document, apparently ancient, coming from the proper repository or custody, and bearing on its face no evident marks of forgery, the law presumes to be genuine, and devolves the opposing party the burden of proving it to be otherwise" (1995, p. 16). He then noted that "this is precisely the case with the Sacred Writings. They have been used in the church from time immemorial, and thus are found in the place where alone they ought to be looked for" (pp.

16-17). Specifically in regard to Ezekiel, that is exactly the case. If the prophet wrote it in the sixth century B.C., his work is exactly where it should be, translated in the Septuagint around the year 250 B.C., and noted to be from the proper time period by Josephus in approximately A.D. 90.

Furthermore, the scholarly world recognized the book's authenticity and original date of composition virtually unanimously for almost 1,900 years. The eminently respected Hebrew scholars Keil and Delitzsch, who wrote in the late 1800s, commented: "The genuineness of Ezekiel's prophecies is, at the present day, unanimously recognized by all critics. There is, moreover, no longer any doubt that the writing down and redaction of them in the volume which has been transmitted to us were the work of the prophet himself" (1982, 9:16). Indeed, Archer noted that no serious objection to the book's integrity was even put forth until 1924 (1974, p. 369).

OBJECTIONS TO EZEKIEL'S
AUTHENTICITY CONSIDERED

In regard to the objections that have been put forth, as Greenleaf noted, the burden of proof concerning the authenticity of Ezekiel lies with those who attempt to consider it inauthentic. Yet, far from proving such, they have put forth tenuous suggestions based on alleged internal inconsistencies. First, these critics have proposed that the work could not have been by one man since some sections are filled with descriptions of doom and destruction, while others resound with hope and deliverance. This alleged inconsistency holds little weight, as Miller noted:

> Of course, this viewpoint is based on purely subjective considerations. No inherent reason exists that forbids a single writer from presenting both emphases. In fact, virtually all the prophets of the Old Testament announce judgment upon God's people and/or their neighbors and then follow that judgment sentence with words of future hope and restoration if repentance is forthcoming.... One must be in possession of a prejudicial perspective before approaching Scripture to come to such a conclusion (1995, p. 138).

The second objection to the integrity of Ezekiel has little more to commend it than the first. The second "proof" of the book's alleged inauthentic nature revolves around the fact that in certain sections, Ezekiel seems to be an eyewitness to events that are happening in Palestine, while at the same time claiming to be writing from Babylon. This objection can be dealt with quickly, in a twofold manner. First, it would be possible, and very likely, that news would travel from the remnant of Israelites still free in Palestine to the captives in Babylon. Second, and more likely, if Ezekiel was guided by divine inspiration, he could have been given the ability to know events in Palestine that he did not see (see Miller, 1995, pp. 138-139). Taking the prophecy of Tyre into account, it is clear that Ezekiel did possess/receive revelation that allowed him to report events that he had not seen and that were yet to take place.

A third objection to Ezekiel's authenticity actually turns out not to be an objection at all, but rather a verification of Ezekiel's integrity. W.F. Albright, the eminent and respected archaeologist, noted that one of C.C. Torrey's "principle arguments against the authenticity of the prophecy" (the book of Ezekiel–KB) was the fact that Ezekiel dates things by the "years of Jehoiachin's captivity" (1948, p. 164). Supposedly, Jehoiachin would not have been referred to as "king" since he was captive in another land and no longer ruled in his own. Until about 1940, this argument seemed to possess some merit. But in that year, Babylonian tablets were brought to light that contained a cuneiform inscription giving the Babylonian description of Jehoiachin as king of Judah, even though he was in captivity (p. 165). Albright concluded by saying: "The unusual dates in Ezekiel, so far from being indications that the book is not authentic, prove its authenticity in a most striking way" (p. 165).

Due to the fact that modern critics have failed to shoulder the burden of proof laid upon them to discredit Ezekiel's integrity and authenticity, Smith rightly stated: "The critical studies of the Book of Ezekiel over the past fifty years or so have largely cancelled each other out. The situation now is much the same as it was prior to 1924 (the work of Hoelscher) when the unity and integrity of the book were generally accepted by the critics" (Smith, 1979, p. 33). Miller correctly concluded: "All theories and speculations which call into question the unity and integrity of the book of Ezekiel are unconvincing.... The most convincing view is the traditional one that sees Ezekiel as the long recognized sixth century Hebrew prophet and author of the Old Testament book which bears his name" (1995, p. 139).

CONCLUSION

So accurate were the prophecies made by Ezekiel that skeptics were forced to suggest a later date for his writings. Yet, such a later date cannot be maintained, and the admission of Ezekiel's accuracy stands as irrefutable evidence of the prophet's divine inspiration. With the penetrating gaze that can only be maintained by the divine, God looked hundreds of years into the future and told Ezekiel precisely what to write so that in the centuries following the predictions, the fulfillment of every detail of the prophet's words could not be denied by any honest student of history. "When the word of the prophet comes to pass, the prophet will be known as one whom the Lord has truly sent" (Jeremiah 28:9). Ezekiel's accurate prophecy adds yet another piece of insurmountable evidence to support the fact that "all Scripture is inspired of God" (2 Timothy 3:16).

CHAPTER 10

MESSIANIC PROPHECY

In hindsight, a good mystery fits together perfectly, like the various pieces of an intricate puzzle that need but one final piece to link the parts that form the completed magnificent panorama. Until that final piece is added, the mystery is virtually impossible to grasp in its entirety. In fact, while the mystery is developing, the inquisitor's greatest challenge is to assess correctly which pieces of information or evidence are of significance and which are the banal elements that add nothing of consequence to the story. Is it important that Mr. Brown forgot his hat at the train station? Does it matter that the water faucet in the kitchen suddenly is not working properly? Inevitably, the astute inquisitor accurately pinpoints those elements in the story that are of great import. The less astute inaccurately labels ordinary events as important, or fails to understand fully events that were of major consequence.

Such is the case when approaching the study of the predicted Messiah, or, as it were, when solving the mystery of the Messiah. Anyone familiar with New Testament writings is quite familiar with the term "mystery" as it is applied to God's plan for the redemption of the human race through the predicted Messiah. Paul wrote concerning this mystery: "But we speak the wisdom of God in a mystery, the hidden wisdom which God ordained before ages for our glory" (1 Corinthians 2:7). In his letter to the Colossians, he stated: "I became a minister according to the stewardship from God which was given to me for you, to fulfill the word of God, the mystery which has been hidden from ages and from generations, but now has been revealed to his saints" (1:25-26). Paul's epistle to the Ephesians contains similar comments: "[I]f indeed you have heard of the dispensation of the grace of God which was given to me for you, how that by revelation He made known to me the mystery...which in other ages was not made known to the sons of men as it has now been revealed by the Spirit to His holy apostles and prophets" (3:3,5).

The New Testament writers identified for us several characteristics of this Messianic mystery: (1) The mystery revolves around the prophesied Messiah and the redemption of mankind; (2) The mystery is one that has been hidden in various ways from all generations of people prior to the time of the New Testament; (3) The various tenets of the mystery are divinely revealed and made known only through divine communication; (4) During the times of the New Testament writers, God revealed the final piece of the mystery to the New Testament writers themselves.

The intention of this discussion is to trace out the various divinely revealed tenets of the Messianic mystery. Upon completion of that task, we must then determine if, in truth, the New Testament writers did possess the final, completing piece of that mystery. We have dealt in other places with the traces of a Savior originating from various sources outside the biblical writings (see Butt and Lyons, 2006, pp. 35-74). Therefore, since the Hebrew Scriptures are renowned for being the most complete repository of Messianic predictions available, we will focus our attention upon them.

OLD TESTAMENT SCRIPTURES

In contemplating the Old Testament, Jewish Scriptures, it would be beneficial for us to consider several important features of the writings. First, the opening eleven chapters of the first book, Genesis, do not relate to the Hebrews only, but to the broader scope of humanity as a whole. These chapters describe the creation of the Universe, the fall of man from his perfect state of innocence, the wickedness of man and the destructive, world-wide Flood, and the repopulation of the Earth. They contain approximately 2,000 years of history, not a year of which necessarily has anything to do with the Jewish nation, any more than with any other nation.

Second, the remainder of the Old Testament, from Genesis 12-Malachi focuses primarily on the descendants of Abraham. Note that the narratives and terms often used to describe these descendants are none too flattering. They are called stubborn, stiff-necked, sinful, rebellious, and a host of adjectives equally as caustic (see Deuteronomy 9:7; Ezekiel 2:3-10; Hosea 4:16). And yet, these descendants of Abraham are the ones responsible for preserving the very Scriptures that repeatedly rebuked them for their idolatrous backsliding from God. Remember, too, that they could have altered and preserved these writings in a more flattering form. From archaeological finds we have learned that other nations surrounding ancient Israel often chose to embellish their history, intentionally excluding derogatory remarks or events concerning themselves.

Why did the Israelites preserve the writings as they did? The answer to this is actually twofold. First, they believed the particular writings that they preserved to be inspired by God. But secondly, each of the 39 books contains a calculated revelation describing some aspect of the coming Messiah, Who, according to these Scriptures, is not only destined to save the nation of Israel, but the entire world. In fact, the reader cannot progress far into the Old Testament writings before he is inundated with descriptions of, and predictions concerning, the coming Messiah.

WERE THE JEWS LOOKING FOR A MESSIAH?

It has been suggested that the ancient Jewish scribes, rabbis, and general population were not really looking for a personal Messiah. Eminently respected Messianic Jewish author David Baron first published his work, *Rays of Messiah's Glory*, in 1886. In that volume, Baron wrote:

> I am aware also that in recent times many intelligent Jews, backed by rationalistic, so-called Christians...deny that there is hope of a Messiah in the Old Testament Scriptures, and assert that the prophecies on which Christians ground such a belief contain only "vague anticipations and general hopes, but no definite predictions of a personal Messiah," and that consequently the alleged

agreement of the gospel history with prophecy is imaginary (2000, p. 16).

In his statements that refute the "non-Messianic" view of Old Testament Scripture, Baron wrote: "Even Maimonides, the great antagonist of Christianity, composed that article of the Jewish creed which unto the present day is repeated daily by every true Jew: 'I believe with a perfect faith that the Messiah will come, and although His coming be delayed, I will await His daily appearance'" (p. 18). He commented further: "Aben Ezra, Rashi, Kimchi, Abarbanel, and almost every other respectable and authoritative Jewish commentator, although not recognizing Jesus as the Messiah, are yet unanimous that a personal Messiah is taught in the Old Testament Scriptures" (pp. 19-20). Baron also noted that only an "insignificant minority of the Jews" had dared to suggest that the Old Testament lacks definitive predictions of a personal Messiah. He then eloquently stated: [W]ith joy we behold the nation [Jews–KB], as such, still clinging to the anchor which has been the mainstay of their national existence for so many ages–the hope of a personal Messiah, which is the essence of the Old Testament Scriptures" (2000, p. 20).

In his volume, *The Messiah in the Old Testament: In Light of Rabbinical Writings*, Risto Santala wrote: "If we study the Bible and the Rabbinic literature carefully, we cannot fail to be surprised at the abundance of Messianic interpretation in the earliest works known to us.... [T]he Talmud states unequivocally: 'All the prophets prophesied only for the days of the Messiah'" (1992, p. 22).

In regard to specific Old Testament prophecies, a plethora of rabbinical commentary verifies that the nation of Israel certainly had in view a coming Messiah. Concerning Genesis 49:10, the noted author Aaron Kligerman wrote: "The rabbis of old, though not agreeing with each other as to the meaning of the root Shiloh, were almost unanimous in applying the term to the Messiah" (1957, pp. 19-20). Immediately after this statement, Kligerman listed the Targum Onkelos, Targum Jerusalem, and the Peshito all as referring to Genesis 49:10 as a Messianic prophecy pointing toward an individual, personal Messiah (p. 20). With reference to Genesis 49:10, David Baron wrote: "With regard to this prophecy, the first thing I want to point out is that **all antiquity agrees in interpreting it of a personal Messiah**. This is the view of the LXX Version [Septuagint–KB]; the Targumim of Onkelos, Yonathan, and Jerusalem; the Talmud; the Sohar; the ancient book of 'Bereshith Rabba;' and among modern Jewish commentators, even Rashi, who says, 'Until Shiloh come, that is King Messiah, Whose is the kingdom'" (2000, p. 258, emp. added).

Concerning the book of Isaiah and the predictive, Messianic prophecy contained within it, Santala stated: "The Messianic nature of the book of Isaiah is so clear that the oldest Jewish sources, the Targum, Midrash and Talmud, speak of the Messiah in connection with 62 separate verses" (1992, pp. 164-165). Santala then, in a footnote, proceeded to list several of those verses, including Isaiah 4:2, 9:5, 10:27, 11:1, 11:6, 14:29, 16:1, 28:5, 42:1, 43:10, 52:13, and 60:1 (p. 165).

The prophecy of Jeremiah contains material that has long been recognized as Messianic in nature. Concerning Jeremiah 23:5-6, David Baron wrote: "There is scarcely any contrary opinion among ancient and modern Jews but that this is a Messianic prophecy" (2000, p. 78).

In truth, statements that verify that the ancient Israelite nation recognized certain passages in the Old Testament as Messianic are legion. Regardless of what a person believes about the identity of the Messiah, it cannot be gainsaid that the nation of Israel, through the influence of the Old Testament writers, has been waiting for His coming.

THE PROTEVANGELIUM

Virtually from the first glimpse of human life on the Earth, traces of the predicted Messiah were divinely revealed to mankind. All too familiar is the tragic story of the fall of man. Under God's gracious care, Adam and Eve were specially designed to suit each other's needs and were ushered into the Edenic Paradise, the joys of which humanity has not seen since nor will see again this side of eternity. God gave the first family only one prohibitory commandment—that they should not eat from the tree of the knowledge of good and evil. If they chose to rebel against this lone prohibition, God informed them that the consequence would be death. Yet despite God's gracious warning, Eve's senses were dulled by her evil desires, and she soon fell prey to the deceitfulness of sin, convincing her husband Adam to join in her rebellion.

Into this scene of shame and sin, God brought judgment upon all parties involved. Death would be the consequence of this sinful action, as well as increased pain in childbirth for the woman and increased hardship and toil for the man. Yet in the midst of God's curse upon the serpent, He included a ray of glorious hope for humanity. To the serpent he said: "And I will put enmity between your seed and her Seed; He shall bruise your head, and you shall bruise His heel" (Genesis 3:15). This brief statement made by God to the serpent concerning the Seed of woman is often referred to as the protevangelium. J.A. Huffman commented on the passage:

> Here the prophecy of a deliverer is unmistakably uttered. Even a temporary bruise, that of the heel, suggesting the apparent, momentary defeat of the deliverer is predicted: but, at the same time, the deliverer's ultimate and final triumph is prophesied, in his bruising of the serpent's head, which means a fatal blow (1956, p. 38).

The Jewish scholar, Aaron Kligerman, noted that three things stand out in this first prediction of the Messiah, "namely that the Deliverer must be–(A) of the *seed of woman* and (B) That He is to be *temporarily hindered* and (C) *Finally victorious*" (1957, p. 13, iltalics in orig.). Kligerman further noted that the ancient rabbinical opinions found in the Palestinian Targum testify "that in Genesis 3:15 there is promised a healing of the bite in the heel from the serpent, which is to take place 'at the end of the days, in the days of King Messiah'" (p. 14). [NOTE: The Targums "are interpretive renderings of the books of Hebrew Scriptures... into Aramaic" (Metzger, 1993, 150:35). Such versions were needed when the major populations of the Jews no longer spoke Hebrew as their primary language. Metzger further explains that the oral Targum began as a simple paraphrase of the text, "but eventually it became more elaborate and incorporated explanatory details." John Stenning, in his detailed article on the Targum, explained that oral Targum was introduced several years prior to the first century A.D. in connection with "the custom of reading sections from the Law at the weekly services in the synagogues" (1911).]

Of the protevangelium, Charles A. Briggs, in his classic work, *Messianic Prophecy*, noted:

> Thus we have in this fundamental prophecy explicitly a struggling, suffering, but finally victorious human race, and implicitly a struggling, suffering and finally victorious son of woman, a second Adam, the head of the race.... The protevangelium is a faithful miniature of the entire history of humanity, a struggling seed ever battling for ultimate victory.... [U]ntil it is realized in the sublime victories of redemption" (1988, p. 77).

Briggs went on to comment that the protevangelium "is the only Messianic prophecy which has been preserved from the revelations made by God to the antediluvian world" (p. 77).

Here, then, is the seminal prophecy made to pave the way for all others that would deal with the coming of the great Deliverer of mankind. Several qualities of this coming Deliverer are readily apparent. First, He will come in human form as the seed of woman. Second, He will defeat the effects of sin brought about by the fall of man and the entrance of sin into the world. Third, He will be hindered in His redemptive activity by the serpent, Satan, who will inflict upon Him a minor wound. Fourth, He will ultimately overcome the wound of Satan and finally triumph. In this first prediction of the Messiah, we catch an underlying theme of a suffering, victorious redeemer—a theme that will be fleshed out in the remaining pages of the Old Testament.

THE SEED OF ABRAHAM

The protevangelium in Genesis 3:15 predicted that the conquering Messiah would belong to the seed of woman, taking on a human form. But that feature alone, admittedly, does not help much in identifying the Messiah, since billions of people have been born of woman. In order for Messianic prophecy to prepare its readers for the actual Messiah, the scope would need to be narrowed.

Such narrowing of the Messianic scope can be seen in God's promise to the patriarch, Abraham. In Genesis 12, the Bible records the fact that God specifically chose Abraham from among all the peoples of the world (Genesis 12:1-3). Through Abraham, God promised that all the nations of the world would be blessed, and that Abraham's descendants would multiply as the sand of the sea and the stars of the sky. As Huffman noted, "It was to Abraham, the son of Terah, a descendant of Shem, that God gave a peculiar promise, one which could not be omitted in any serious effort to trace the Messianic hope" (1956, p. 41). For many years, this promise of progeny remained unfulfilled due to the fact that Abraham's wife, Sarah, was barren. In order to "help" God fulfill His promise, Abraham and Sarah devised a plan by which Abraham could have a child. Sarah sent her handmaid, Hagar, to serve as a surrogate wife to Abraham. As a result of this union, Hagar conceived and gave birth to a child named Ishmael.

In Genesis 17, God renewed His covenant with Abraham and instructed Abraham to institute circumcision as a sign of the covenant. In Genesis 17:19, God informed Abraham that Sarah would have a son named Isaac. In an interesting conversation with God, Abraham petitioned God to let Ishmael be the son of promise and the heir of the covenant that God made. Yet God insisted that Ishmael was not the son of promise and that the promise of all nations being blessed through Abraham's descendants would not pass through Ishmael, but would be fulfilled only through Isaac. God said: "But My covenant I will establish with Isaac, whom Sarah shall bear to you at this set time next year" (Genesis 17:21).

James Smith, in writing about God's promise to bless all nations through Abraham, noted that this promise "has Messianic implications. Both the Church Fathers and Jewish Rabbis so interpreted it" (1993, p. 47). Aaron Kligerman concurred when he wrote about God's promise to Abraham: "This is more than the promise of 'The Hope of a Prosperous Era.' It is a promise of the coming of a 'Personal Messiah'" (1957, pp. 17-18). At this point in human history, then, the Messianic implications fall to the descendants of Isaac. It is important not to miss the significance of the Messianic hope through Abraham and Isaac. The scope of the Messiah has been narrowed from all other peoples and nations of the world, to a single nomadic family.

And yet, not just to Abraham's family in its entirety, but to only one of Abraham's sons—Isaac.

But the picture becomes even clearer with the birth of the twin sons of Isaac and Rebekah. Because of abnormalities with her pregnancy, Rebekah went to inquire of the Lord about her situation. To answer her questions, the Lord said: "Two nations are in your womb, two peoples shall be separated from your body; one people shall be stronger than the other, and the older shall serve the younger" (Genesis 25:23). Concerning this passage, Briggs noted: "This prediction breaks up the seed of Isaac into two nations, assigns the headship with the blessing to Jacob, and makes Edom subject to him" (1988, p. 90). The fact that the promised Messiah would come through Jacob's descendants becomes increasingly clear throughout the Genesis narrative that tells the stories of Jacob and Esau. God confirmed the promise to Jacob in Genesis 28:14, when He said to the patriarch: "Also your descendants shall be as the dust of the earth; you shall spread abroad to the west and the east, to the north and the south; and **in you and in your seed all the families of the earth shall be blessed**" (emp. added). The picture of the Messiah continues to become increasingly focused: The seed of woman, the seed of Abraham, the seed of Isaac, the seed of Jacob.

TWO MESSIAHS: A SUFFERING SERVANT AND REIGNING KING

Throughout the Old Testament, various Messianic passages refer to a majestic, glorious King Who will reign over a never-ending kingdom. Yet, at the same time, other Messianic prophecies depict a suffering Messiah Who will bear the guilt and sin of the entire world. Because these two aspects of Messianic prophecy seem contradictory, many in the ancient Jewish community could not understand how such diverse prophetic sentiments could be fulfilled in a single individual. Due to this conundrum, ancient and modern Jews have posited the idea that two Messiahs would come: one would be the suffering Servant, while the other would be the glorious King.

Concerning this separation of the Messiah into two different individuals, John Ankerberg and his colleagues John Weldon and Walter Kaiser wrote:

> [T]hey (early Jewish rabbis–KB) could not reconcile the statements that so clearly spoke of a suffering and dying Messiah with those verses in other passages that spoke of a triumphant and victorious Messiah. What is important to note is that they did recognize that both pictures somehow applied to the Messiah. But they assumed it was impossible to reconcile both views in one person. Rather than seeing one Messiah in two different roles, they saw two Messiahs–the suffering and dying Messiah, called "Messiah ben Joseph," and the victorious conquering Messiah, called "Messiah ben David" (1989, pp. 57-58).

Jewish rabbi Robert M. Cohen stated:

> The rabbis saw that scripture portrayed two different pictures of King Messiah. One would conquer and reign and bring Israel back to the land by world peace and bring the fullness of obedience to the Torah. They called him Messiah ben David. The other picture is of a servant who would die and bear Israel's sin that they refer to as the "leprous

one" based on Isaiah 53 (Cohen, n.d.; also see Parsons, 2006).

It is evident, from the rabbinical view of two Messiahs, that the themes of suffering and regal authority were so vividly portrayed in Old Testament Messianic prophecy that both themes demanded fulfillment. To suggest two Messiahs provided such a fulfillment. However, the dual Messianic idea failed to comprehend the actual nature of Messianic prophecy, and missed a primary facet of the Messianic personality: that the Messiah would be **both** a suffering Servant and a majestic King. As Huffman rightly observed: "The theme of Messianism is composed of two inseparable strands or threads–the scarlet and the golden, or the suffering and the reigning, or the priestly and the royal" (1956, p. 7). To misunderstand or miss either of these two interwoven threads would be to miss the Messiah completely.

Genesis 49:10—Shiloh

The Lord kept His promise to Jacob and multiplied his descendants exceedingly. His twelve sons and their wives and children escorted him to Egypt to live in the land of Goshen at the behest of Joseph, who had been elevated in Egypt as the Pharaoh's chief advisor. As Jacob neared the end of his rather long life (over 130 years, Genesis 47:9), he gathered his sons around his death bed, and stated: "Gather together, that I may tell you what shall befall you in the last days" (Genesis 49:1). Following this introductory statement, Jacob proceeded to address each of his sons and bestow blessings (or in some cases, curses) on his descendants.

In the midst of his final speech, in his blessing on Judah, Jacob stated: "The scepter shall not depart from Judah, nor a lawgiver from between his feet, until Shiloh comes; and to Him shall be the obedience of the people" (Genesis 49:10). The Messianic nature of this statement has long been recognized and discussed in ancient Jewish circles. David Baron wrote:

> With regard to this prophecy, the first thing I want to point out is that **all antiquity agrees in interpreting it of a personal Messiah**. This is the view of the LXX. Version; the Targumim of Onkelos, Yonathan, and Jerusalem; the Talmud; the Sohar; the ancient book of "Bereshith Rabba;" and among modern Jewish commentators, even Rashi, who says, "Until Shiloh come, that is King Messiah, Whose is the kingdom" (2000, p. 258, emp. added).

Aaron Kligerman added: "The rabbis of old, though not agreeing with each other as to the meaning of the root Shiloh, were almost unanimous in applying the term to the Messiah" (1957, pp. 19-20). Santala, in his discussion of several of the oldest Jewish documents available, wrote:

> Targum Onqulos says of Judah's scepter that it will not depart *"until the Messiah comes, he who has the power to reign."* Targum Jonathan puts it that the verse refers to *"the age of the Messiah-King, the King who will come as the youngest of his children."* Targum Yerushalmi speaks of the 'time' when *"the Messiah-King will come"* (1992, p. 50, italics in orig.).

Much commentary and debate surrounds the "Shiloh" prophecy found in Genesis 49:10. It is often viewed as an indication of the time that the Messiah should arrive on the scene. As can be deduced from

Kligerman's quote, the actual origin and exact meaning of the word "Shiloh" are disputed in many scholarly circles. Yet, despite the controversy in reference to this prophecy, the one aspect of it that stands out is the central idea that this is a Messianic prophecy. As such, it narrows the identity of the Messiah even further to a descendant, not just of Abraham, Isaac, and Jacob, but to the house of Judah.

The Son of David

Of all the monarchs that possessed the throne of Israel, none is as storied as King David. From his youth he proved himself to be a courageous, valiant warrior who trusted in the Lord. He was described as a man after God's own heart (1 Samuel 13:14). He wrote many of the Psalms, and ushered in a united kingdom that paved the way for the majestic reign of his son, Solomon.

David's relationship to the Messiah is a rather interesting one. First, Jewish antiquity recognized the fact that Messiah would be the Son of David. Santala commented: "*Tradition ascribes 73 of the 150 psalms to King David.* In the Rabbinic literature the Messiah is constantly referred to as the 'Son of David.' For this reason, everywhere the future blessing of the house of David is described, the Sages saw Messianic material" (1992, p. 109, italics in orig.).

Such Messianic sentiments in regard to David find their seminal origin in the promise made by God to David through the prophet Nathan. In 2 Samuel 7, the text narrates the events that lead to this promise. David had become a great king and his reign had spread far and wide. Due to his love for the Lord, he wanted to show honor to God by building a glorious temple in which the Ark of the Covenant could be housed. He mentioned his idea to the prophet Nathan, who immediately encouraged the building plans. But soon after Nathan had told David to do all that was in his heart, God conveyed to Nathan that He did not want David to build a temple. Instead, God would commission David's son, Solomon, to construct the magnificent edifice. Yet, in God's message to David, He promised: "And your house and your kingdom shall be established forever before you. Your throne shall be established forever" (2 Samuel 7:16).

In later psalms, the promise of David's descendant reigning over an eternal Kingdom is expanded and given more substance. Psalm 89 contains several Messianic aspects, not the least of which is the following statement: "I have made a covenant with My chosen, I have sworn to My Servant David: 'Your seed I will establish forever, and build up your throne to all generations'" (vss. 3-4). Psalm 132 contains a very similar statement: "The Lord has sworn in truth to David; He will not turn from it: 'I will set upon your throne the fruit of your body. If your sons will keep My covenant and My testimony which I shall teach them, their sons also shall sit upon your throne forevermore" (vss. 11-12).

Along with the various inspired psalmists, other Old Testament writers noted the Messianic lineage through David and his throne. One of the most memorable of all Messianic predictions from the Old Testament, Isaiah 9:6-7, mentioned the Messianic reign upon the throne of David:

> For unto us a Child is born, unto us a Son is given;
> and the government will be upon His shoulder.

And His name will be called Wonderful, Counselor,
Mighty God, Everlasting Father, Prince of Peace.
Of the increase of His government and peace
there will be no end, upon the throne of David
and over His kingdom, to order it and establish it
with judgment and justice from that time forward,
even forever. The zeal of the Lord of hosts will
perform this.

Yet, along with the fact that the Messiah was to be
of the seed of David and reign on His throne, at least
one Psalm places David in a subservient position to
this majestic Messianic ruler. Psalm 110 opens with
the statement: "The Lord said to my Lord, 'Sit at My
right hand, till I make Your enemies Your footstool'"
(Psalm 110:1). In regard to Psalm 110, Briggs noted:
"The 110th Psalm is in the form of an utterance from
Jahveh respecting the son of David. It is therefore a
prediction that unfolds the prediction of Nathan" (1988,
p. 132). Walter Kaiser, in his discussion of Psalm 110,
wrote: "While the external evidence that this psalm
is Messianic is large, the internal evidence is just as
overwhelming" (1995, p. 94). In reference to the Messiah mentioned in the first verse, Kaiser stated: "That
unnamed Lord is a royal person, for he was invited
to 'sit at [God the Father's] right hand....' If the God of
the universe invited this other Sovereign to take such
a distinguished seat alongside himself, then we may
be sure he was no one less than the promised Messiah,
invited to participate in the divine government of the
world" (p. 94).

Psalm 110 adds an interesting aspect to the character and position of the Messiah. Not only would the
Messiah be born from the seed of David and reign on

the throne of David, He also would be exalted to a position far above David, to such an extent that David called him "Lord" in Psalm 110. David's statements in this psalm not only speak to the pre-existence of the Messiah before David, but also to the pre-eminence that the Messiah would assume.

With these details, the portrait of the Messiah becomes increasingly sharp. He was to come from the seed of woman and crush the power of Satan. He was to be of the seed of Abraham, Isaac, Jacob, Judah and now David. He would rule on the throne of David, yet He existed before David and was so preeminent that David called Him Lord. And there would be no end of His glorious, majestic kingdom.

THE SUFFERING SERVANT

Anyone who reads the Old Testament would be hard pressed to miss the idea of the Messiah's glorious regal prominence. Yet the idea that this same Messiah must also suffer is equally apparent. The protevangelium in Genesis 3:15 makes reference to this suffering in the statement about the heel of the Seed of women being bruised, but it does not include the details of this suffering. The theme of suffering introduced in Genesis 3:15 is expanded in the remainder of the Old Testament.

Isaiah 52:13-53:12

The passage of Scripture found in Isaiah 52:13-53:12 stands as a somber reminder of the horrendous suffering that the Messiah would endure. The text mentions that He would be highly exalted and extolled (52:13). And yet His appearance would be marred more than any man (52:14). He would not be physically attractive (53:2), and He would be despised and rejected by men, familiar with sorrows and grief (53:4). He would be perfect and without sin (53:9), and yet He would be beaten, suffer, and die for the sins of the Lord's people (53:5-6,11). This suffering Servant would be killed among the wicked, but buried among the rich (53:8-9). Yet, in spite of His death (or even because of it), He would be numbered among the great and divide the spoil with the strong (53:12).

Needless to say, this picture of the Messiah seems to stand in stark contrast to the glorious King on David's throne. As has been mentioned, this contrast has caused some to concoct two Messiahs to accommodate the prophecies. Still others have attempted to discount Messianic prophecies such as Isaiah 52:13-53:12. Some have suggested that this passage of Scripture is not Messianic in nature, but that the servant under discussion represents the collective nation of Israel. Along these lines, David Baron noted: "Modern Jews, in common with a number of rationalistic so-called Christians, are trying hard these days to weaken the Messianic application of this remarkable prophecy" (2000, p. 225). James Smith stated:

> The Messianic interpretation of Isaiah 53 was acknowledged by Jewish authorities until the Middle Ages. Almost all Christian leaders until the beginning of the nineteenth century saw in this passage a clear picture of the suffering, death and resurrection of the Messiah. Jews and some Christian scholars now hold primarily to the collective view of the Servant: The Servant is Israel as a whole, or

the remnant. The traditional view, however, has
much to commend it (1993, p. 307).

That the ancient Jewish community, and the bulk of
scholars for the last 2,000 years, have recognized Isaiah
53 as a prophecy concerning a personal, individual Messiah cannot be questioned. Baron correctly commented
regarding this sentiment: "That until recent times this
prophecy has been almost universally received by Jews
as referring to Messiah is evident from Targum Yonathan, who introduces Messiah by name in chapter lii
13, from the Talmud ('Sanhedrin," fol. 98, b); and from
Zohar, a book which the Jews as a rule do not mention
without the epithet 'holy...'" (2000, p. 226).

The recent view that Isaiah 53 refers to the nation
of Israel not only garners little (if any) support from
ancient Jewish commentators, but it collapses under the
scrutiny of critical examination. The foremost objection to the view that Israel collectively is the Servant
in Isaiah 53 is the fact that the Servant is described as
perfect and sinless (53:9), not deserving the punishment
that He willingly accepts for the sins of God's people.
No one remotely familiar with the nation of Israel as
portrayed in the Old Testament would dare suggest
that they were sinless. From their first few steps out of
Egypt and into freedom they began to provoke God
and bring judgment upon themselves. On numerous
occasions the Old Testament depicts the Israelites' sin of
such a rebellious nature that God executes thousands of
them. One fundamental aspect of an atoning sacrifice
in Old Testament literature was its condition of spotless
perfection. No nation of mere mortal men, including
the ancient Israelite nation, could suffice as an atoning

sacrifice for sins, as the Servant does in Isaiah 53. Nor could a sinful nation make another group of people "righteous" as the Lord's Servant would. Furthermore, the Servant of the Lord is depicted as being stricken for "transgressions of my people." If the Servant was collectively depicted as the nation of Israel, then who would be the Lord's people in 53:8? [NOTE: For a more complete refutation of Israel as the Servant of the Lord in Isaiah 53, see Baron, 2000, pp. 225-251.]

Indeed, the evidence points overwhelmingly to the fact that Isaiah 53 stands as one of the most poignant portrayals in all of the Old Testament of an individual, suffering Messiah. As Smith correctly noted: "The Servant of the Lord here is portrayed in a strongly individualistic way. It takes rich imagination or strong prejudice to see the Servant here as a symbol for Israel, the remnant, the prophets, or any other group" (p. 1993, 307). Kaiser similarly commented: "Undoubtedly, this is the summit of OT prophetic literature. Few passages can rival it for clarity on the suffering, death, burial, and resurrection of the Messiah (1995, p. 178).

VARIOUS SPECIFIC MESSIANIC PROPHECIES

In addition to the broad strokes portraying the Messiah as a reigning king and suffering servant, there are a host of more specific, detailed prophecies that relate to His coming. In regard to the number of Messianic prophecies, Santala wrote. "It is estimated that the Old Testament contains altogether some 456 prophecies concerning Christ. Of these 75 are to be found in the Pentateuch, 243 in the Prophets and 138 in the

'Writings' and Psalms" (1992, p. 149; cf. Free and 1992, p. 241).

Space prohibits a listing of all of these prophecies, but a representative sampling is appropriate. The Messiah was to be born in Bethlehem in Judea (Micah 5:2) of a virgin (Isaiah 7:14). He was to be betrayed by a friend (Psalm 41:9) for thirty pieces of silver (Zechariah 11:13). The Lord's Ruler would come into Jerusalem riding on the foal of a donkey (Zechariah 9:9). He would be buried with the rich (Isaiah 53:9). During His suffering, His clothes would be distributed to those who cast lots for them (Psalm 22:18). His attackers would pierce Him (Zechariah 12:10). Even though His physical suffering would be severe, His bones would not be broken (Psalm 34:20). And in spite of His death, His physical body would not experience decay (Psalm 16:10). This small sampling of specific prophetic details is only a fraction of the many Old Testament prophecies that exist. The prophecies were specifically designed to be an efficient mechanism by which the Jewish community could recognize the Messiah when He arrived.

WHO IS THE MESSIAH?

When all of the pieces of the Messianic puzzle are put together, one individual stands out as the only person who fulfilled every single prophecy in minute detail–Jesus Christ. The life and activities of Jesus Christ as recorded in the New Testament blend the theme of a regal monarch and a suffering servant into one magnificent portrait of the triumphant Jesus Who was the sacrificial lamb at His death on the cross, and Who became the triumphant Lion of Judah in His resurrection from the grave. The lineage of Jesus Christ is meticulously traced in order to show that He qualified as the Seed of Abraham, of Isaac, of Jacob, of Judah, and of David (see Matthew 1 and Luke 3:23-38). The narrative detailing His birth verifies that He was born in Bethlehem of Judea, from which city the Messiah would arise (Luke 2:1-7). The birth narrative also intricately portrays the pre-existence of Jesus before time began, fulfilling the prophecy that the Messiah would come before King David. Furthermore, Jesus did, in fact, enter Jerusalem riding on the foal of a donkey (Matthew 21:1-11).

The New Testament narratives depicting the death of Jesus Christ verify that He was betrayed by His friend and sold for exactly 30 pieces of silver (Matthew 24:14-16). At His death His bones were not broken, soldiers cast lots for His garments, and His side was pierced with a spear (John 19:33-37 and Matthew 27:35). During His suffering, He was numbered with the transgressors, as Isaiah 53 predicted, by being crucified between two thieves, and at His death He was buried in the tomb of a wealthy man as was also foretold (Matthew 27:57). This type of verification could continue for many pages. The life of Jesus Christ of Nazareth, as depicted in the New Testament documents, was designed to fulfill the Messianic prophecy of the Old Testament.

Due to this overwhelming congruence of the life of Jesus Christ with the predictive Messianic prophecy of the Old Testament, some have suggested that Jesus was an imposter who was able, by masterful manipulation, to so artificially organize His life as to make it look like He was the Messiah. Such a contention cannot be reasonably maintained in light of the fact that many of the prophecies were far beyond His control. Obviously, it would be impossible for a person to arrange where he would be born. Furthermore, it would be impossible to coordinate events so that He could ensure that He was buried in the tomb of a rich man or crucified among thieves. How could the betrayal price of Judas be manipulated by Jesus? And how, pray tell, would Jesus have managed to arrange it so that soldiers cast lots for His clothing? The idea that Jesus manipulated events to make it appear as if He was the Messiah not only is indefensible, but it also speaks to the fact that Jesus obviously was the fulfillment of the Old Testament, Messianic prophecies.

Others have objected to Jesus as the Messiah based on the idea that the New Testament documents are not reliable, and were artificially concocted to describe things that Jesus never really did. This objection also falls flat in light of the actual evidence. It cannot be denied that the New Testament has proven itself to be the most reliable book in ancient history. When it records people, places, and events that are checkable using archaeological means, those people, places, and events invariably prove to be factual and historic (see chapter 4). Again, the abundant evidence verifies that the New Testament is accurate and factual. Many of the Messianic prophecies documented in the New Testament do not describe anything inherently miraculous. There was nothing miraculous about Jesus being buried in a rich man's tomb. Nor was there anything miraculous about Jesus riding into Jerusalem on the foal of a donkey, or being betrayed by His friend for

30 pieces of silver. These events are, if not ordinary, at least very plausible, everyday events that theoretically could have happened to anybody. And yet, due to the fact that such everyday events had been predicted about the Messiah **hundreds of years before the arrival of Jesus**, the fulfillment of the events becomes one of the most amazing miracles recorded in the Bible. It is no wonder that Jesus, the apostles, and the early church used fulfilled Messianic prophecy as one of their foundational pillars of proof and evangelistic tools.

APPEALING TO PROPHECY

Even a slight familiarity with the New Testament texts sufficiently demonstrates the idea that Jesus, the apostles, and the other New Testament writers used the Old Testament Messianic prophecies as one of their main apologetic tools to prove the deity and Messianic role of Jesus Christ.

The Writers of the Gospel Accounts Applied Messianic Prophecy to Jesus Christ

The Gospel writers repeatedly peppered their narratives of the life and actions of Jesus Christ with allusions, quotes, and Messianic prophecies from the Old Testament, which they applied to Jesus. Matthew 1 includes the Messianic prophecy taken from Isaiah 7:14 in which a virgin is predicted to bear a son. Matthew applies this virgin-birth prophesy to the birth of Jesus Christ. In chapter 2, Matthew references Micah 5:2, in which the birth city of the Messiah is named, again applying the prophecy to Jesus. In Matthew 3, the Bible writer notes that John the Baptizer was the fulfillment of Isaiah's prophecy in 40:3, indicating that John was the forerunner of the Messiah which, again, is Jesus Christ. Matthew 4:15-16 references another Messianic prophecy that discusses the land of Zebulun and Naphtali, again applying the prophecy to Jesus Christ. Looking, then, at the first four chapters of the book of Matthew, one is forcefully struck with the fact that one of the Bible writer's primary apologetic tools used to confirm that Jesus was (and is) the Messiah was a fervent appeal to Messianic prophecy as fulfilled in the life and actions of Jesus. Furthermore, Matthew's pattern of applying Old Testament, Messianic prophecy to Jesus continues throughout the remainder of his account.

Mark's gospel account, although not as replete with such prophecies, nevertheless includes appeals to Messianic prophecy and applies those prophecies to Jesus. Mark chapter 1 begins with quotations from Malachi 3 and Isaiah 40 that predict the forerunner of the Messiah. Mark applied these passages to John the Baptizer as the forerunner of Jesus Christ. Furthermore, during the crucifixion account as recorded in Mark, the Bible writer noted that Jesus was crucified between two thieves, and then he commented, "So the Scripture was fulfilled which says, 'And He was numbered with the transgressors'" (15:28). In addition, Mark included instances in which Jesus applied Messianic prophecy to Himself.

As with Matthew and Mark, Luke and John also included numerous Messianic prophecies and appeal to them as proof of the deity of Jesus Christ. Luke chapter three cites the prophecy from Isaiah 40 concerning the Messianic forerunner and applies it to John the Baptizer, the forerunner of Christ. John does the same in 1:23. During Jesus' triumphal entry into Jerusalem, John records that Jesus rode into the city sitting on a donkey. John then commented on the situation by saying: "as it is written: Fear not, daughter of Zion; behold, your King is coming, sitting on a donkey's colt." His reference was a clear appeal to the Messianic nature of this prophecy found in Zechariah 9:9. Again, in John 12:37-38, the Bible writer refers to a Messianic prophecy in Isaiah 53:1, and applies its fulfillment to the ministry of Jesus. During the crucifixion of Christ, John records that the soldiers cast lots for Jesus' clothing. John then references Psalm 22:18 as a Messianic prophecy: "They divided My garments among them, and for my clothing they cast lots."

Only a few of the many Messianic prophetic references in the gospel accounts have been documented here. Yet, even with this small sampling, the reader is struck with the clear conclusion that the gospel writers appealed to Old Testament, Messianic prophecy as proof of the deity of Christ.

Jesus' Appeal to Prophecy as it Applied to Him

On multiply occasions, Jesus directed His listeners to certain Messianic Old Testament Scriptures, and applied those Scriptures to Himself. Luke records an incident in the life of Jesus in which He visited a synagogue on the Sabbath in His hometown of Nazareth. While in attendance there, Jesus read a passage from Isaiah 61:1-2, and commented to those in attendance that the particular Scripture He had just read was fulfilled in their hearing.

During His arrest in the Garden of Gethsemane, Jesus addressed those who had come to arrest Him, asking them why they did not apprehend Him while He was with them daily teaching in the temple. He then stated: "But the Scriptures must be fulfilled" (Mark 14:49). His statement implied that this deed they were doing was a fulfillment of Old Testament Scriptures as they related to His Messianic role.

Again, in Luke 24, the resurrected Jesus appeared to two of His disciples on the road to Emmaus. They treated Him as a stranger, because they did not recognize Him. Upon striking up a conversation with Jesus, they began to discuss the events of Christ's death and burial in Jerusalem only a few days earlier. After the disciples related the events of the women at the empty tomb, Jesus began to speak to them with these words: "O foolish ones, and slow of heart to believe in all that the prophets have spoken! Ought not the Christ to have suffered these things and to enter into His glory" (Luke 24:25-26). The verse following Jesus' statement explains: "And beginning at Moses and all the Prophets, He expounded to them in all the Scriptures the things concerning Himself."

A few verses later, in the same chapter, Jesus appeared to several more of His disciples and applied the Old Testament prophecies to His activities again: "Then He said to them, 'These are the words which I spoke to you while I was still with you, that all the things must be fulfilled which were written in the Law of Moses and the Prophets and the Psalms concerning Me" (Luke 24:44). Such statements made by Jesus show that one of the main lines of evidence that He used to establish

His identity as the Messiah was the application of Old Testament Messianic prophecy to Himself.

Messianic Prophecy Applied to Jesus in the Book of Acts

The recorded writings and sermons of the apostles after the ascension of Jesus are replete with appeals to Messianic prophecy as proof of the Messianic identity of Jesus Christ. In the first recorded gospel sermon on the Day of Pentecost, Peter explained to those in Jerusalem that the resurrection of Christ was a fulfillment of the Messianic prophecy uttered by David in Psalm 16:8-11 (which says that the Lord would not allow His Holy One to see corruption). In Act 3, Peter addressed another multitude of those dwelling in Jerusalem. In his sermon, he stated: "But those things which God foretold by the mouth of all His prophets, that Christ would suffer, He has thus fulfilled" (vs. 18). In that same sermon, Peter referred his audience back to Deuteronomy 18, in which Moses had foretold the coming of a prophet like himself, which Peter applied to Jesus (as did Stephen in his sermon in Acts 7:37). In the next chapter, Peter is arrested and allowed to speak to the high priest and his family. In Peter's statements to these leaders, he again referred back to the Old Testament, quoted Psalm 118:22 about the stone that was rejected by the builders, and applied the prophecy to Jesus.

In one of the most memorable conversion accounts, Philip the evangelist is called to meet with an Ethiopian treasurer on the road to Gaza. As Philip approached, the Eunuch was reading a passage from Isaiah 53. Upon their meeting, the Eunuch asked Philip about the prophecy, wondering whether the prophet was speaking of himself or someone else. From that text, the Bible says that Philip preached Jesus to the Eunuch, applying the passage from Isaiah as a Messianic prophecy with its fulfillment in the person of Christ (Acts 8:26-40). In another memorable conversion account, Peter visited the house of Cornelius and preached the Gospel to him and all his household. Included in Peter's message was the following statement concerning Jesus: "To Him **all the prophets witness**, that through His name, whoever believes in Him will receive remission of sins" (Acts 10:43, emp. added).

As one continues through the book of Acts, it becomes evident that Paul often appealed to prophecy as evidence of Christ's deity. In Acts 13, while preaching to those in the synagogue in Antioch of Pisidia, he commented that those responsible for killing Jesus did so because they did not know "the voices of the Prophets which are read every Sabbath" (Acts 13:27). In the same verse he concluded that because of their ignorance of the prophetic message, the murderers of Christ actually fulfilled the prophecies concerning Jesus in their abuse of Him. Paul further quoted from Psalm 2:7, Isaiah 55:3, and Psalm 16:10, noting these Old Testament passages as Messianic prophecy and applying them to Jesus Christ.

In a separate sermon, delivered much later, Paul stood before King Agrippa and told him that Jesus is the Christ. In his oratory to Agrippa, Paul acknowledged that the king was "expert in all customs and questions which have to do with the Jews" (Acts 26:3). Paul further noted that in his teachings concerning Jesus as the Messiah, he was telling Agrippa "no other things than those which the prophets and Moses said would come" (26:22). In his concluding remarks, Paul said to the king, "King Agrippa, do you believe the prophets? I know that you do believe." Agrippa responded to Paul with these words: "You almost persuade me to become a Christian" (Acts 26:27-28).

Examples of Messianic prophecy applied to Jesus by the early propagators of Christianity as recorded in the book of Acts could easily be multiplied further. These few instances suffice to establish the fact that, throughout the book of Acts, predictive prophecy as it applied to Jesus as the Messiah stood as one of the foundational pillars upon which Christianity was based and spread.

Messianic Prophecy Applied to Jesus in the Epistles

Without providing an exhaustive study of every instance of Old Testament prophecy applied to Jesus in the epistles, this brief section will provide enough examples to establish the fact that the epistles, in similar fashion to the other books of the New Testament, rely heavily upon Messianic prophecy to establish the deity of Jesus Christ.

The book of Romans begins with a section discussing the Gospel of God, "which He promised before through His prophets in the Holy Scriptures, concerning His Son Jesus Christ our Lord, who was born of the seed of David according to the flesh..." (1:2-3). In the book of Galatians, Paul refers back to the promise made to Abraham, that through the seed of the patriarch all nations would be blessed. Paul then applies that promise to Jesus, stating that Jesus is the Seed of

Abraham through whom the world would receive the blessing of Abraham (Galatians 3:15-18). The writer of the book of Hebrews opens by discussing the merits of Christ, applying many Old Testament passages such as Psalm 2:7 and Psalm 110:1 to Jesus. In Hebrews 5, the writer argues the case that Jesus is a priest after the order of Melchizedek as prophesied in Psalm 110:4. He repeats these sentiments in 7:17 and 7:21.

The epistles of 1 and 2 Peter contain numerous examples of such prophetic application to Jesus. One of the most potent passages along these lines is found in 1 Peter 1:10-12, in which Peter wrote:

> Of this salvation the prophets have inquired and searched carefully, who prophesied of the grace that would come to you, searching what, or what manner of time, the Spirit of Christ who was in them was indicating when He testified before-hand the sufferings of Christ and the glories that would follow. To them it was revealed that, not to themselves, but to us they were ministering the things which now have been reported to you through those who have preached the gospel to you by the Holy Spirit sent from heaven—things which angels desire to look into.

In 1 Peter 2:6, the apostle applies Isaiah 28:16 and Psalm 118:22 to Christ, describing Him as the chief cornerstone rejected by the builders. Again in 1 Peter 2:22, the apostle applies Isaiah 53:9 to Jesus, referring to the fact that the Messiah would be sinless as was Jesus.

It becomes readily obvious, then, that the New Testament writers and apostles frequently referred to Old Testament Messianic prophecy and applied the fulfillment of such prophecies to the life, death, and resurrection of Christ. It is impossible to deny that one of the main lines of reasoning upon which the Christian faith was founded from its inception is the idea that Jesus Christ fulfilled the Old Testament prophecies that looked forward to a coming Messiah.

CONCLUSION

In the Old Testament, it is almost as if we have a satellite picture from space of the Messiah many thousands of miles away, yet with each new prophecy, the picture continues to move nearer, until at last we are able to view a complete close-up of the Messiah–Jesus Christ. As the distinguished Hebrew scholar Charles Briggs noted: "In Jesus of Nazareth the key of the Messianic prophecy of the Old Testament has been found. All its phases find their realization in His unique personality, in His unique work, and in His unique kingdom. The Messiah of prophecy appears in the Messiah of history" (1988, p. 498).

In Acts 8:26-40, Philip the evangelist approached the Ethiopian who was riding in a chariot reading the Old Testament Scriptures. As Philip approached, he heard the man reading a section from Isaiah 53 in which the sufferings of the Messiah are depicted. Upon entering into a conversation with Philip, the man asked Philip, "[O]f whom does the prophet say this, of himself or of some other man?" Immediately after this question, the Bible says that Philip "opened his mouth, and beginning at this Scripture, preached Jesus to him" (Acts 8:35). In truth, Jesus is the sum total of every Old Testament Messianic prophecy ever

AFTERWORD

For more than 3,500 years, God has providentially preserved His inspired Word in the 66 books of the Bible. The message preserved in those books provides humanity with all things that pertain to life and godliness (2 Peter 1:3). In fact, so complete is that message, that it perfectly equips the man of God for all good works (2 Timothy 3:16). Yet, among those who profess to believe that the Bible is God's Word, it has become a common practice to avoid following certain biblical commands, based on the idea that such commands were specifically for the individuals at the time of the writing, and do not have broader application to those of us who are reading the text in a modern-day setting. The idea, then, is that God is not really talking to us through the Bible today, but was talking only to "those" people "back then."

Jesus had something to say about this very idea. On one memorable occasion, the Sadducees came to Jesus, testing Him with questions pertaining to the resurrection. In their minds, they had concocted an unanswerable scenario. If a woman had seven husbands in this life, they questioned, whose wife would she be in the resurrection? Jesus, knowing their wickedness and their ignorance of the Scripture, explained that "in the resurrection they neither marry nor are given in marriage" (Matthew 22:30). He then said to the Sadducees, "But concerning the resurrection of the dead, have you not read what was spoken to you by God, saying, 'I am the God of Abraham, the God of Isaac, and the God of Jacob'? God is not the God of the dead, but of the living" (Matthew 22:31-32, emp. added).

Notice that Jesus quoted to the Sadducees a segment of Scripture that was taken from the Pentateuch (Exodus 3:6). The text was written almost 1,500 years before this group of Sadducees even existed. In the text, God was speaking directly to Moses, who had a much different culture than those of the first-century Jews. And yet, even with such a lengthy time span and major cultural differences involved, Jesus stated clearly that God was talking to His first-century audience.

We must realize that God speaks to us today through His inspired Word, just as He spoke to the Sadducees almost 2,000 years ago. While it is true that some things in Scripture must be analyzed in their cultural setting, and the division between the Old Testament and New Testament must be recognized, it is extremely dangerous to jettison applicable commands and divine principles based on the idea that they no longer apply to us. Even though our culture may drift far from many of the biblical teachings, those teachings have not changed, and will not change due to ever-waffling cultural trends. Regardless of cultural shifts, it will never be right to jettison God's applicable commands based on the idea that such commands were solely for someone else in some other time. As the psalmist wrote about God in the long ago, "The entirety of Your word is truth, and every one of Your righteous judgments endures forever" (Psalm 119:160). If you want to listen to God speak to you today, read His inspired Word, "which is able to build you up and give you an inheritance among all those who are sanctified" (Acts 20:32).

REFERENCES

Abbott, Jacob (1850), *History of Cyrus the Great* (New York: Harper Brothers).

"About the Bible" (2005), [On-line], URL: http://www.ibs. org/bibles/about/19.php.

Adler, Jerry and Anne Underwood (2004), "Search for the Sacred," *Newsweek*, 144[9]:37-41, August 30.

Albright, W.F. (1948), "The Old Testament and Archaeology," *Old Testament Commentary*, ed. Herbert Alleman and Elmer Flack (Philadelphia, PA: Muhlenberg Press).

Albright, W.F. (1968), *Yahweh and the Gods of Canaan* (Garden City, NY: Doubleday).

Ancient Egyptian Medicine: The Papyrus Ebers (1930), (Chicago, IL: Ares Publishers).

"Ancient Phoenicia" (no date), [On-line], URL: http://gorp. away.com/gorp/location/africa/phonici5.htm.

"Ancient Tyre (Sour)" (no date), [On-line], URL: http://ancientneareast.tripod.com/Tyre.html.

Ankerberg, John, John Weldon, and Walter Kaiser (1989), *The Case for Jesus the Messiah* (Chattanooga, TN: John Ankerberg Evangelistic Association).

Archer, Gleason L. Jr. (1974), *A Survey of Old Testament Introduction* (Chicago, IL: Moody), revised edition.

Archer, Gleason L. Jr. (1982), *Encyclopedia of Bible Difficulties* (Grand Rapids, MI: Zondervan).

Ash, Anthony L. (1987), *Jeremiah and Lamentations* (Abilene, TX: Abilene Christian University Press).

Barfield, Kenny (1995), *The Prophet Motive* (Nashville, TN: Gospel Advocate).

Barker, Dan (1992), *Losing Faith In Faith–From Preacher to Atheist* (Madison, WI: Freedom from Religion Foundation).

Baron, David (2000 reprint), *Rays of Messiah's Glory* (Jerusalem, Israel: Kern Ahvah Meshihit).

Benjamin of Tudela (no date), "Traveling in Jerusalem," [On-line], URL: http://chass.colostate-pueblo.edu/history/seminar/benjamin.htm.

Benjamin of Tudela (1907), *The Itinerary of Benjamin of Tudela* (New York, NY: The House of the Jewish Book), [On-line], URL: http://chass.colostate-pueblo.edu/history/seminar/benjamin/benjamin1.htm.

"Best Selling Author Worldwide" (2002), [On-line], URL: http://answers.google.com/answers/threadview?id=14.

Blaiklock, E.M. (1984), *The Archaeology of the New Testament* (Grand Rapids, MI: Zondervan), revised edition.

Bonz, Marianne (1998), "Recovering the Material World of the Early Christians," [On-line], URL: http://www.pbs.org/wgbh/pages/frontline/shows/religion/maps/arch/recovering.html.

Boyd, Robert (1969), *A Pictorial Guide to Biblical Archaeology* (New York: Bonanza).

Briggs, Charles A. (1988 reprint), *Messianic Prophecy: The Prediction of the Fulfillment of Redemption through the Messiah* (Peabody, MA: Hendrickson).

Bruce, F.F. (1953), *The New Testament Documents–Are They Reliable?* (Grand Rapids, MI: Eerdmans), fourth edition.

Bruce, F.F. (1990), *The Book of Acts* (Grand Rapids, MI. Eerdmans), third revised edition.

Bryant, Dewayne (2007), "Discovering the Truth About 'The Lost Tomb of Jesus,'" *Reason & Revelation*, 27[5]:33-

39, [On-line], URL: http://www.apologeticspress.org/articles/3322.

Butt, Kyle (2002), "James, Son of Joseph, Brother of Jesus," [On-line], URL: http://www.apologeticspress.org/articles/495.

Butt, Kyle and Eric Lyons (2006), *Behold the Lamb of God* (Montgomery, AL: Apologetics Press).

"Carlos' Tragic and Mysterious Illness: How Carlos Almost Died by Eating Contaminated Raw Oysters" (2003), U.S. Food and Drug Administration, [On-line], URL: http://www.cfsan.fda.gov/~acrobat/vvfoto.pdf.

Clarke, Adam (no date), *Clarke's Commentary on the Bible* (Nashville, TN: Abingdon).

Cohen, Robert M. (no date), "Why I Know Yeshua is the Jewish Messiah," [On-line], URL: http://www.imja.com/Atonem.html.

"Cyprus," McClintock, John and James Strong (1968 reprint), *Cyclopaedia of Biblical, Theological, and Ecclesiastical Literature* (Grand Rapids, MI: Baker).

Davis, George T.B. (1931), *Fulfilled Prophecies that Prove the Bible* (Philadelphia, PA: Million Testaments Campaign).

"The Death of George Washington, 1799," (2001), *EyeWitness to History*, [On-line], URL: http://www.eyewitnesstohistory.com.

Dever, William (2001), *What Did the Bible Writers Know and When Did They Know It?* (Grand Rapids, MI: Eerdmans).

Dilion, Denise (2005), "Fugu: The Deadly Delicacy," *Welcome Magazine*, [On-line], URL: http://www.welcome-moldova.com/articles/fugu.shtml.

Eaves, Thomas F. (1980), "The Inspired Word," *Great Doctrines of the Bible*, ed. M.H. Tucker (Knoxville, TN: East Tennessee School of Preaching).

Edersheim, Albert (no date), *The Bible History–Old Testament*, (Grand Rapids, MI: Eerdmans).

"Faith" (2006), *Merriam-Webster Online Dictionary*, [On-line], URL: http://www.m-w.com/dictionary/Faith.

Fausset, A.R. (1990 reprint), "Jeremiah," *A Commentary on the Old and New Testaments*, ed. Robert Jamieson, A.R. Fausset, and David Brown (Grand Rapids, MI: Eerdmans).

Finegan, Jack (1959), *Light from the Ancient Past* (Princeton, NJ: Princeton University Press), second edition.

Finegan, Jack (1992), *The Archeology of the New Testament* (Princeton, NJ: Princeton University Press), revised edition.

Finegan, Jack (1998), *Handbook of Biblical Chronology* (Peabody, MA: Hendrickson).

Finkelstein, Israel and Neil Silberman (2001), *The Bible Unearthed* (New York: Simon & Schuster).

Fitch (1954), "Isaiah," *The New Bible Commentary*, ed. F. Davidson (Grand Rapids, MI: Eerdmans).

Fleming, Wallace B. (1966), *The History of Tyre* (New York, NY: AMS Press).

Free, Joseph P. and Howard F. Vos (1992), *Archaeology and Bible History* (Grand Rapids, MI: Zondervan).

Freeman, Hobart (1968), *An Introduction to the Old Testament Prophets* (Chicago, IL: Moody).

Frey, Rebecca J. (no date), "Thuja," [On-line], URL: http://health.enotes.com/alternative-medicine-encyclopedia/thuja.

Gaussen, L. (1850), *Theopneustia: The Plenary Inspiration of the Holy Scriptures* (London: Johnstone & Hunter).

Geisler, Norman L. and Ronald M. Brooks (1990), *When Skeptics Ask* (Wheaton, IL: Victor).

Geisler, Norman L. and William E. Nix (1986), *A General Introduction to the Bible* (Chicago, IL: Moody), revised edition.

"God Facts" (no date), [On-line], URL: http://www.wwj. org.nz/gfacts.php.

Greenbaum, Dorothy (2006), "Say 'Yes' to Circumcision," [On linc], URL: http://www.beliefnet.com/story/8/story_813_1.html.

Greenlee, J. Harold (1985), *Scribes, Scrolls, and Scriptures* (Grand Rapids, MI: Eerdmans).

Greenleaf, Simon (1995), *The Testimony of the Evangelists* (Grand Rapids, MI: Kregel Classics).

Guthrie, Donald (1970), *New Testament Introduction* (Downers Grove, IL: Inter-Varsity Press), third edition.

Haley, John (1876), *An Examination of the Alleged Discrepancies of the Bible* (Grand Rapids, MI: Baker, 1977 reprint).

Hanson, K.C. (2002), *Sennacherib Prism*, [On-line], URL: http://www.kchanson.com/ANCDOCS/meso/senn-prism1.html.

Harrison, R.K. (1969), *Introduction to the Old Testament* (Grand Rapids, MI: Eerdmans).

Harrison, R.K. (1982), "Heal," *International Standard Bible Encyclopedia*, ed. Geoffrey W. Bromiley (Grand Rapids, MI: Eerdmans), revised edition.

Hendrix, Eddie (1976), "What About Those Copyist Errors?" *Firm Foundation*, 93[14]:5, April 6.

Herodotus, (1972 reprint), *The Histories*, trans. Aubrey De Sélincourt (London: Penguin).

Hoerth, Alfred J. (1998), *Archaeology and the Old Testament* (Grand Rapids, MI: Baker).

Holman, Thomas (1926), "Prophecy Vindicated by Volney," *New Testament Christianity*, ed. Z.T. Sweeney (Columbus, IN: NT Christianity Book Fund).

Holt, L.E. and R. McIntosh (1953), *Holt Pediatrics* (New York: Appleton-Century-Crofts), twelfth edition.

Huffman, J.A. (1956), *The Messianic Hope in Both Testaments* (Butler, IN: Higley Press).

Hughes, J.J. (1986), "Paulus, Sergius," *International Standard Bible Encyclopedia*, ed. Geoffrey W. Bromiley (Grand Rapids, MI: Eerdmans), revised edition.

"Human Rabies Often Caused by Undetected, Tiny Bat Bites" (2002), *Science Daily*, [On-line], URL: http://www.science-daily.com/releases/2002/05/020506074445.htm.

Hyatt, James Phillip (1956), *The Interpreter's Bible*, ed. George A. Buttrick (Nashville, TN: Abingdon).

"Hyssop" (no date), [On-line], URL: http://www.taoherbfarm.com/herbs/herbs/hyssop.htm.

"Inspiration" (no date), *Merriam-Webster On-line Dictionary*, [On-line], URL: http://www.m-w.com/dictionary/Inspiration.

Jackson, Wayne (1991), *Isaiah: God's Prophet of Doom and Deliverance* (Abilene, TX: Quality).

Jackson, Wayne (1996), "Zopyrus the Persian," *Christian Courier*, 32[7]:27, November.

Jacobs, Joseph and J. Frederick McCurdy (2002), "Moabite Stone," *Jewish Encyclopedia*, [On-line], URL: http://www.jewishencyclopedia.com/view.jsp?artid=680&letter=M.

Jeremias, Alfred (1911), *The Old Testament in the Light of the Ancient East* (New York: Putnam's Sons).

"Johann Gutenberg" (2006), [On-line], URL: http://en.wikipedia.org/wiki/Johann_Gutenberg.

Josephus, Flavius (1987 edition), *Antiquities of the Jews*, in *The Life and Works of Flavius Josephus*, trans. William Whiston (Peabody, MA: Hendrickson).

Josephus, Flavius (1987 edition), *Against Apion*, in *The Life and Works of Flavius Josephus*, trans. William Whiston (Peabody, MA: Hendrickson).

Kaiser, Walter (1995), *The Messiah in the Old Testament* (Grand Rapids, MI: Zondervan).

Katzenstein, Jacob (1973), *The History of Tyre* (Jerusalem: The Schocken Institute for Jewish Research).

Keil, C.F. and F. Delitzsch (1982 reprint), *Commentary on the Old Testament—Ezekiel and Daniel* (Grand Rapids, MI: Eerdmans).

Keith, Alexander (1840), *Evidence of the Truth of the Christian Religion Derived From Prophecy* (Edinburgh, Scotland: William Shyte).

Kenyon, Sir Frederic (1951 reprint), *Handbook to the Textual Criticism of the New Testament* (Grand Rapids, MI: Eerdmans), second edition.

King, Leonard W. (1919), *A History of Babylonia and Assyria* (London: Chatto & Windus).

King, Philip J. and Lawrence E. Stager (2001), *Life in Biblical Israel*, ed. Douglas A. Knight, (Louisville, KY: Westminster John Knox Press).

Kligerman, Aaron (1957), *Old Testament Messianic Prophecy* (Grand Rapids, MI: Zondervan).

Knight, Kevin (2002), "The Fathers of the Church," [Online], URL: http://www.newadvent.org/fathers/.

Koldewey, Robert (1914), *The Excavations at Babylon* (London: Macmillan).

Laughlin, John C.H. (2000), *Archaeology and the Bible* (New York: Routledge).

Layard, Austen H. (1856), *The Ruins of Nineveh and Babylon* (New York: Harper).

LeMaire, André (1994), "House of David Restored in Moabite Inscription," *Biblical Archaeology Review*, 20[3]:30-37, May/June.

Lightfoot, Neil R. (2003), *How We Got the Bible* (Grand Rapids, MI: Baker).

Luckenbill, Daniel D. (1989), *Ancient Records of Assyria and Babylon* (London: Histories and Mysteries of Man).

Lyons, Eric (2003), *The Anvil Rings: Volume 1* (Montgomery, AL: Apologetics Press).

Lyons, Eric (2005a), *The Anvil Rings: Volume 2* (Montgomery, AL: Apologetics Press).

Lyons, Eric (2005b), "'Breaking Bread' on the 'First Day' of the Week" [On-line], URL: http://www.apologeticspress. org/articles/343.

Lyons, Eric and Zach Smith (2003), "Mosaic Authorship of the Pentateuch," *Reason & Revelation*, 23[1]:1-7.

Macht, David I. (1953), "An Experimental Pharmacological Appreciatioin of Leviticus XI and Deuteronomy XIV," *Bulletin of the History of Medicine*, 27:5, September-October.

Massengill, S.E. (1943), *A Sketch of Medicine and Pharmacy* (Bristol, TN: S.E. Massengill).

Mazar, Amihai (1992), *Archaeology of the Land of the Bible* (New York: Doubleday).

McClintock, John and James Strong (1969 reprint), *Cyclopedia of Biblical, Theological, and Ecclesiastical Literature* (Grand Rapids, MI: Baker).

McGarvey, J.W. (no date), *New Commentary on Acts of Apostles* (Delight, AR: Gospel Light).

McGarvey, J.W. (1886), *Evidences of Christianity* (Cincinnati, OH: Guide Printing).

McGarvey, J.W. and Philip Y. Pendleton (no date), *The Fourfold Gospel* (Cincinnati, OH: The Standard Publishing Foundation).

McGrew, Roderick (1985), *Encyclopedia of Medical History* (London, England: Macmillan Press).

McKinsey, C. Dennis (1995), *The Encyclopedia of Biblical Errancy* (Amherst, NY: Prometheus).

McLeod, Lianne (2007), "*Salmonella* and Reptiles," [On-line], URL: http://exoticpets.about.com/cs/reptiles/a/reptsalmonella.htm.

McMillen, S.I. and David Stern (2000), *None of These Diseases* (Grand Rapids, MI: Revell), third edition.

McRay, John (1991), *Archaeology and the New Testament* (Grand Rapids, MI: Baker).

Metzger, Bruce (1968), *The Text of the New Testament* (New York: Oxford University Press).

Metzger, Bruce (1993), "The Jewish Targums," *Bibliotheca Sacra,* 150:35ff. January, [On-line], URL: http://www.bible-researcher.com/aramaic4.html.

Millard, Alan (1985), *Treasures From Bible Times* (Oxford, England: Lion Publishing).

Miller, Dave (1995), "Introduction to Ezekiel," *Major Lessons from the Major Prophets*, ed. B.J. Clarke (Pulaski, TN: Sain Publications).

Miller, Stephen M. and Robert V. Huber (2004), *The Bible: A History: The Making and Impact of the Bible* (Intercourse, PA: Good Books).

Moorey, P.R.S. (1991), *A Century of Biblical Archaeology* (Louisville, KY: Wesminster/John Knox Press).

Morris, Brian (2006), "Benefits of Circumcision," [On-line], URL: http://www.circinfo.net/#why.

Negev, Avraham and Shimon Gibson (2001), *Archaeological Encyclopedia of the Holy Land* (New York: Continuum).

Nuland, Sherwin B. (2003), *The Doctor's Plague* (New York: Atlas Books).

Nicoll, W. Robertson (no date), *The Expositor's Greek Testament* (Grand Rapids, MI: Eerdmans).

"Ossuary" (2001), *Archaeological Encyclopedia of the Holy Land*, ed. Avraham Negev and Shimon Gibson (New York: Continuum).

Paché, Rene (1971), *The Inspiration and Authority of Scripture* (Grand Rapids, MI: Eerdmans).

Parsons, John (2006), "Hebrew Names of God: The Mashiach as Revealed in the Tanakh," [On-line], URL: http://www.hebrew4christians.com/Names_of_G-d/Messiah/messiah.html.

Plumptre, E.H. (1959 reprint), *Ellicott's Commentaries* (Grand Rapids, MI: Zondervan).

Price, Randall (1997), *The Stones Cry Out* (Eugene, OR: Harvest House).

Pritchard, James B., ed. (1958a), *The Ancient Near East: An Anthology of Texts and Pictures* (Princeton, NJ: Princeton University Press).

Pritchard, James B. (1958b), *Archaeology and the Old Testament* (Princeton, NJ: Princeton University Press).

Ramsay, William M. (1915), *The Bearing of Recent Discovery on the Trustworthiness of the New Testament* (Grand Rapids, MI: Baker, 1975 reprint).

Ramsay, William M. (1897), *St. Paul the Traveller and the Roman Citizen* (Grand Rapids, MI: Baker, 1962 reprint).

Rawlinson, George (1950 Reprint), "Isaiah," *The Pulpit Commentary* (Grand Rapids, MI: Eerdmans).

Ritmeyer, Kathleen and Leen Ritmeyer (1992), "Reconstructing Herod's Temple Mount in Jerusalem," *Archaeology and the Bible: Archaeology in the World of Herod, Jesus and Paul*, ed. Hershel Shanks and Dan P. Cole (Washington, D.C.: Biblical Archaeology Review).

Rollin, Charles (1857), *Ancient History* (New York: Harper & Brothers).

Rufus, Quintus Curtius (2001), *The History of Alexander,* trans. John Yardley (New York, NY: Penguin).

"*Salmonella* Bacteria and Reptiles" (2007), ARAV, [On-line], URL: http://www.arav.org/SalmonellaOwner.htm.

Sanderson, Edgar, J.P. Lamberton, and John McGovern (1900), *The World's History and Its Makers* (Chicago, IL: Universal History Publishing).

Santala, Risto (1992), *The Messiah in the Old Testament: In the Light of Rabbinical Writings*, trans. William Kinnaird (Jerusalem, Israel: Keren Ahvah Meshihit).

Septuagint (1998 reprint), (Peabody, MA: Hendrickson).

Shanks, Hershel (1987), "Jeremiah's Scribe and Confidant Speaks from a Hoard of Clay Bullae," *Biblical Archaeology Review*, 13[5]:58-65, September/October.

Shanks, Hershel (1995), *Jerusalem: An Archaeological Biography* (New York: Random House).

Shanks, Hershel (1996), "Fingerprint of Jeremiah's Scribe," *Biblical Archaeology Review*, 22[2]:36-38, March/April.

Shanks, Hershel (2004), "The Seventh Sample," [On-line], URL: http://www.bib-arch.org/bswbbreakingseventh.html.

Siculus, Diodorus (1963), *Library of History*, trans. C. Bradford Welles (Cambridge, MA: Harvard University Press).

Skinner, J. (1963), "Isaiah: I-XXXIX," *The Cambridge Bible for Schools and Colleges* (Cambridge, England: Cambridge University Press).

Slater, T. (2007), "Lying," [On-line], URL: http://www.newadvent.org/cathen/09469a.htm.

Smith, James (1979), *Ezekiel* (Joplin, MO: College Press).

Smith, James (1993), *What the Bible Teaches about the Promised Messiah* (Nashville, TN: Thomas Nelson).

"Soapmaking" (no date), [On-line], URL: http://www.itdg.org/docs/technical_information_service/soapmaking.pdf.

"Spa Essential Oils" (2005), [On-line], URL: http://www.mysticthai.com/spa/essential_oil.asp.

Stenning, John F. (1911), "Targum," *Encyclopedia Britannica*, [On-line], URL: http://www.bible-researcher.com/aramaic3.html.

Stern, Ephraim (2001), *Archaeology and the Land of the Bible: The Assyrian, Babylonian, and Persian Periods (732-332 B.C.E.)*, (New York: Doubleday).

Thompson, Bert (1999), *The Global Flood of Noah* (Montgomery, AL: Apologetics Press).

Thompson, Bert and Sam Estabrook (2004), "Does the Story of Rahab Mean that God Condones Lying?" [On-line], URL: http://www.apologeticspress.org/articles/535.

Thompson, J.A. (1962), *The Bible and Archaeology* (Grand Rapids, MI: Eerdmans).

Thompson, J.A. (1987), *The Bible and Archaeology* (Grand Rapids, MI: Eerdmans), third edition.

Till, Farrell (no date), "Prophecies: Imaginary and Unfulfilled," [On-line], URL: http://www.infidels.org/library/modern/farrell_till/prophecy.html.

"Tyre" (2006), *Columbia Encyclopedia,* [On-line], URL: http://yahooligans.yahoo.com/reference/encyclopedia/entry?id=48355.

Unger, Merrill (1962), *Archaeology and the New Testament* (Grand Rapids, MI: Zondervan).

Vos, Howard (1988), "Belshazzar," *Baker Encyclopedia of the Bible,* ed. Walter A. Elwell (Grand Rapids, MI: Baker).

Wegner, Paul (1999), *The Journey from Text to Translations* (Grand Rapids, MI: Baker Academic).

Wiseman, D.J. (1979), "Jeremiah," *The New Layman's Bible Commentary,* ed. G.C.D. Howley, F.F. Bruce, and H.L. Ellison (Grand Rapids, MI: Zondervan).

"Worldwide Scripture" (1999), [On-line], URL: http://www.biblesociety.org/wr_340/sdr_1998.htm.

Wright, G. Ernest (1960), *Biblical Archaeology* (Philadelphia, PA: Westminster).

Xenophon (1893 Edition), *Cyropaedia,* trans. J.S. Watson and Henry Dale (London: George Bell & Sons).